DEMOCRACY AND
DEMOCRATIZATION

DILEMMAS IN WORLD POLITICS

Series Editor

George A. Lopez, University of Notre Dame

Dilemmas in World Politics offers teachers and students of international relations a series of quality books on critical issues, trends, and regions in international politics. Each text examines a "real world" dilemma and is structured to cover the historical, theoretical, practical, and projected dimensions of its subject.

EDITORIAL BOARD

FORTHCOMING

International Human Rights, Second Edition, Jack Donnelly
Southern Africa in World Politics, Janice Love
Russia and the World, Andrew W. Kuchins

SECOND EDITION

DEMOCRACY AND DEMOCRATIZATION

■ ■ ■

Processes and Prospects in a Changing World

Georg Sørensen

University of Aarhus

Westview Press
A Member of Perseus Books, L.L.C.

Dilemmas in World Politics Series

Copyright © 1993, 1998 by Westview Press, A Member of Perseus Books, L.L.C.

Published in 1998 in the United States of America by Westview Press, 5500 Central Avenue, Boulder, Colorado 80301-2877, and in the United Kingdom by Westview Press, 12 Hid's Copse Road, Cumnor Hill, Oxford OX2 9JJ

A CIP catalog record for this book is available from the Library of Congress.
ISBN 0-8133-9984-X

The paper used in this publication meets the requirements of the American National Standard for Permanence of Paper for Printed Library Materials Z39.48-1984.

10   9   8   7   6   5   4

For Lisbet and Mathilde

Contents

ix

□ □ □

Tables and Figures

Tables

Figures

□   □   □

Preface

The first edition of this book appeared in 1993; this second edition revises and updates the argument. The ambition remains the same: to evaluate the current prospects for democracy and democratization. The thematic structure of the book is unchanged, and the most significant additions are the following: Chapter 2 has a new section on prospects for democracy as we approach the millennium; Chapter 3 has been extended with a section on economic performance in the current democratic transitions; and Chapter 5 has been substantially revised to include an evaluation of the possibilities for further democratic consolidation.

I am grateful for much positive response on the first edition from professors and students, including feedback from referees and from Chung-in Moon, who made valuable suggestions on this second edition. I also thank friends and colleagues for their help and encouragement. Series editor George Lopez started this project by inviting me to submit a book proposal on democracy and democratization. Comments from Frances Hagopian and several members of the Dilemmas editorial board helped improve the proposal. Jennifer Knerr and Rachel Quenk from Westview were always ready with advice and support as the project moved along. Jørgen Elklit, Hans-Henrik Holm, Hans-Jørgen Nielsen, Ole Nørgaard, and Palle Svensson read the manuscript, or parts of it, and provided extensive comments that made the first edition a better book. Comments from Westview's two anonymous reviewers of the manuscript were also very useful. Jonna Kjær aided in preparing the final version of the manuscript. Special thanks to Beverly LeSuer, whose expert editorial input significantly improved the readability of the book. Libby Barstow guided it through the final production stage. The second edition has benefited from the generous assistance of Adina Popescu and the wonderful skills of Jonna Kjær in preparing the revised manuscript. Ryan Goldberg safely saw the second edition through production, and Allison Aydelotte was a fine copy editor. Any shortcomings that remain are my responsibility. Finally, I am grateful, once again, for the constant support and encouragement of my wife, Lisbet.

Georg Sørensen

□   □   □

Acronyms

ASEE	authoritarian state elite enrichment regime
CCP	Chinese Communist party
CSCE	Conference on Security and Cooperation in Europe
DDR	Deutsche Demokratische Republik
EU	European Union
GDP	gross domestic product
GNP	gross national product
HDI	Human Development Index
IMF	International Monetary Fund
NATO	North Atlantic Treaty Organization
NGO	nongovernmental organization
NIC	newly industrializing country
OECD	Organization for Economic Cooperation and Development
PPP	purchasing power parities
TNC	transnational corporation
TPLF	Tigrean People's Liberation Front
UN	United Nations
UNDP	United Nations Development Programme

□   □   □

Introduction

A statement often repeated nowadays, both in scholarly circles and in the mass media, is that democracy has made great progress in the world in recent years. The reasons for the statement are simple: In a brief period of time, a large number of countries have commenced a process of democratization. In Eastern Europe, the totalitarian systems are being replaced by democracies; in Africa, the one-party systems headed by strongmen, personally in charge of the state, are challenged by opposition forces exploiting newly gained political liberties; in Latin America, the military dictatorships began crumbling several years ago; in many Asian countries, authoritarian systems are moving—or being forced to move—in a democratic direction.

The swift progress of democracy in many countries has raised hopes for a better world; the expectations are that democracy will not only promote political liberties and other human rights but will also lead to rapid economic development and increased welfare as well as to international relations characterized by peaceful cooperation and mutual understanding. In this book, we will examine the prospects for these great expectations. A necessary first step is to clarify the concept of democracy. This is done in Chapter 1, which introduces different views of democracy, discusses ways of measuring democracy, and identifies the countries that presently qualify as democratic. Next, we need to know whether democracy is advancing in a sustainable fashion. This issue is the theme of Chapter 2. A model is introduced that demonstrates that the process of **democratization**—that is, the movement from authoritarian to democratic forms of rule—is a lengthy one involving different phases. The major part of the chapter is devoted to the formulation of four propositions, each of which spells out an important characteristic of democracy's degree of progress and sustainability. Following this groundwork, we are ready to ask about the domestic and international consequences of democracy. Chapter 3 concentrates on possible domestic consequences for economic development, welfare, and human rights. Chapter 4 turns to the international consequences of democracy: Will it pave the way for a more peaceful and cooperative world? Finally, Chapter 5 considers the future of democracy and democratization against the background of an optimistic and a pessimistic scenario.

In one sense it is true, then, that democracy has made great progress in the world in recent years. We shall see, however, that the way in which democratization has occurred calls into question whether democratic advancement will continue and whether potential positive effects of democracy will be forthcoming. This is the central dilemma surrounding the current transitions toward democracy. Chapters 2, 3, and 4 further investigate particular aspects of this dilemma. Chapter 2 emphasizes that the processes of democratization in recent years are frail openings with democracy still restricted in many ways and with no guarantees of further democratic progress. Chapter 3 argues that economic development and welfare improvement will not necessarily be forthcoming from these fragile democracies. Indeed, there may be a trade-off between democratic stability and welfare progress. Chapter 4 asserts that a more peaceful world as a result of the current democratizations—although a theoretical possibility—is by no means assured. In short, current democratic advancement is taking place in a way that may well jeopardize continued democratic progress.

The book concludes with a chapter on the future of democracy, followed by discussion questions for each chapter and a list of recommended readings for students interested in further study of democracy and democratization.

ONE

□ □ □

What Is Democracy?

Democracy is a form of government in which the people rule. The concrete way in which this form of government should be organized and the question of which conditions and preconditions it requires have been intensely debated for several centuries. Indeed, the early contributions to this discussion go back to ancient Greece. It is my contention that in order to understand democracy and its present position in the world, one must have an awareness of the most important debates about the meaning of democracy; a notion of the core features of democracy relevant for today's world; and an understanding of how economic, social, and cultural conditions affect the quality of democracy. Thus, each of these elements is addressed in this chapter. The aim is merely to introduce the important issues; references will be given to sources with in-depth treatments.

The term democracy comes from the combination of two Greek words: *demos* (people) and *kratos* (rule). The definition "rule by the people" may sound innocently straightforward, but it immediately raises a number of complex issues. The most important ones were aptly summarized in a recent report:

- who are to be considered 'the people'?
- what kind of participation is envisaged for them?
- what conditions are assumed to be conducive to participation? Can the disincentives and incentives, or costs and benefits, of participation be equal?
- how broadly or narrowly is the scope of rule to be construed? Or, what is the appropriate field of democratic activity?
- if 'rule' is to cover 'the political', what is meant by this? Does it cover (a) law and order? (b) relations between states? (c) the economy? (d) the domestic or private sphere?
- must the rules of 'the people' be obeyed? What is the place of obligation and dissent?

- what mechanisms are created for those who are avowedly and actively 'non-participants'?
- under what circumstances, if any, are democracies entitled to resort to coercion against some of their own people or against those outside the sphere of legitimate rule?[1]

It readily appears that a discussion of democracy must involve not only the *theory* about possible ways of organizing rule by the people but also the *philosophy* about what ought to be (that is, the best ways of constructing government) and an understanding of *practical experiences* with the ways in which government has been organized in different societies at different times.

Such considerations are often interwoven in a highly complex manner. At the same time, the most significant contributions to the deliberations about democracy have one important element in common: They have been set against the context of contemporary society as those who have made these contributions perceive it. The debate about democracy therefore has an inbuilt dynamic: It develops and grows to incorporate new aspects and dimensions when the societal context—or the analyst's perception of it—changes.

Thus, Plato's critique of democracy in Athens was set against what he saw as the decline of the city, its defeat in the war with Sparta, and the decay of morality and leadership. In Athens, democracy meant the rule by the poor majority. People could do pretty much as they liked; there was no respect for authority in the family, in schools, or elsewhere. Eventually, Plato reasoned, laws would not be respected but would be seen as attacks on the freedom of the people. This situation would lead to **anarchy** (the absence of political authority) and chaos, paving the way for tyranny (rule by a single dictator). Plato's solution was to recommend rule by the wise, trained, and educated—that is, the philosophers.[2]

Aristotle voiced similar criticisms of democracy, which he also saw as a form of government devoted only to the good of the poor. Developing a position taken by Plato in his later writings, Aristotle argued for some room for popular influence, for example in the making of laws. Such considerations pointed toward a combination of monarchy and democracy, a "mixed state"[3] where a separation of powers ensured a balance of forces between the main groups in society.

With the decline of Athens, the debate about democracy was put on hold for a very long time. In the feudal system of the Middle Ages, power was not vested in elected bodies; it was based on rank that could be attained only through inheritance or by force. "No popular movement, however enraged, would think that its aims could be achieved by getting the vote. And in the nations and independent city-states of the later Middle Ages also, power was not to be sought in that way."[4]

A new body of thought on democracy, based on modern society, did not emerge until the nineteenth century, although its beginnings can be traced to the Renaissance and Niccolò Machiavelli (1469–1527). During this span of time from the Renaissance to the nineteenth century, ideas about democracy took shape in the context of the development of modern, industrial-capitalist society. A large number of highly diverse contributions to the debate about democracy were made during this period, but it is not possible or necessary to give an exhaustive account of them here. The intention in what follows is more modest: to reach a conception of the core features of democracy in the modern sense and to point out main areas where the content and conditions of this conception are still debated.

LIBERAL DEMOCRACY AND ITS CRITICS

Liberalism developed in opposition to the medieval, hierarchical institutions, the despotic monarchies whose claim to all-powerful rule rested on the assertion that they enjoyed divine support. Liberalism attacked the old system on two fronts. First, the liberalists fought for a rollback of state power and the creation of a sphere of **civil society** where social relations, including private business, nonstate institutions, family, and personal life, could evolve without state interference. "Gradually, liberalism became associated with the doctrine that individuals should be free to pursue their own preferences in religious, economic and political affairs—in fact everything that affected daily life."[5] An important element in this regard was the support of a market economy based on the respect for private property.

The second element of early liberalism was the claim that state power was based not on natural or supernatural rights but on the will of the sovereign people. Ultimately, this claim would lead to demands for democracy—that is, for the creation of mechanisms of representation that assured that those who held state power enjoyed popular support. Yet the creation of such mechanisms was not a primary concern of early liberalism. The tradition that became liberal democracy was liberal first (aimed at restricting state power over civil society) and democratic later (aimed at creating structures that would secure a popular mandate for holders of state power). Even when the focus was on democracy, the liberals had various reservations. They feared that democracy would impede the establishment of a liberal society.[6] In a sense the development of liberal democratic thinking evolved around the settling of the complex relationship between these two elements.

The unfolding of thinking on liberal democracy has been instructively summarized by C. B. Macpherson in three different models that he called (1) protective democracy, (2) developmental democracy, and (3) equilibrium democracy.[7] Instead of presenting these models in detail, I will include elements from them in a discussion of more recent debates and critiques with the aim of identifying some of the important issues that have been raised in the different stages of thinking about democracy.

The earliest model of liberal democracy, derived around 1820, builds on contributions from Jeremy Bentham and James Mill. Macpherson called it protective democracy because of the model's preoccupation with the protection of citizens from government and its attempts to ensure that governors would pursue policies in accordance with the interests of citizens as a whole. The way to such protection was seen as universal franchise. The vote gave political power; "one person, one vote" provided self-protection because the rulers could be removed.

In practice, however, Bentham and Mill were willing to accept severe restrictions in the right to vote; women and large sections of the working classes did not enjoy this privilege.[8] Their cause was more liberal than democratic: The aim was to restrict the sphere of politics, especially that of governmental activity and institutions. Civil society should be left to itself, meaning that such issues as "the organization of the economy or violence against women in marriage (rape) are thought of as non-political, an outcome of 'free' private contracts in civil society, not a public issue or a matter for the state."[9]

This concern with negative freedom, that is, freedom of the citizens from pervasive political authority, was echoed some 150 years later in the reflections of the so-called New Right or neo-liberalists. Their preoccupation was with the rollback of a state that keeps expanding its regulatory and redistributive activities in the name of general welfare and social justice.

The leading figure of the New Right, Friedrich von Hayek, makes a sharp distinction between liberalism and democracy. He calls the former a doctrine about what the law ought to be and the latter a doctrine about the manner of determining what will be the law.[10] For Hayek democracy is of only secondary importance. The highest political end is liberty, which can be achieved only if there are strict limits on the activities of governments. Government intervention in civil society must aim at protecting life, liberty, and estate, which basically means creating the best possible framework for the operation of the free market. There can be no room, for example, for redistributive measures because they would jeopardize the free choice of individuals in the free market.[11]

In this view democracy is desirable as a mechanism for securing that the majority will decide what the law should be. It is vital, however, that democratic majorities respect the limitations on government activity. If they do not, democracy will be in conflict with liberty, and if that is the case, Hayek is "not a democrat."[12]

In summary, it is possible to point to both very early and very recent contributions in the liberal democratic tradition whose primary concern is with the restriction of political authority over citizens. Liberty is individual freedom in the realm of civil society. Democracy can be a means of achieving this end but is not the end itself. If there is a democratic core in this way of thinking, it is the principle of the political equality of citizens. In what follows it will appear that this principle can lead in a quite different direction from the one taken by the proponents of protective democracy and can result in a much more central and positive role for democracy.

*   *   *

John Stuart Mill (1806–1873), the son of James Mill, was more enthusiastic about democracy than his father was. The younger Mill saw democracy as an important element in free human development. Participation in political life could lead toward the "highest and harmonious expansion of individual capacities."[13] At the same time, J. S. Mill shared one of the basic assumptions of the protective democrats: The maximum freedom of citizens required a limitation on the scope of the state's activity. His vision was one of representative government in combination with a free-market economy.

Thus, in important ways J. S. Mill followed familiar liberal views concerning the restriction of the scope of government and governmental activity. With regard to enfranchisements, it can even be said that he took a step backward. His father had argued for universal franchise, at least in principle; but J. S. Mill recommended a system of **plural voting** (one in which some members of the electorate have more votes than others) in order to give the "wiser and more talented" more votes than "the ignorant and less able."[14] It is in two other respects that the younger Mill was more democratic than his father. First, in the moral dimension, he saw participation in the political process as a way to liberty and self-development. The importance of participation has been stressed by other thinkers both before and after Mill, as we shall see in a moment. Second, J. S. Mill directly confronted a number of inequalities in mid-nineteenth-century English society that he considered obstacles to the democratic process. He severely criticized the subjection of women and pointed to the need for complete equality between the sexes as a precondition for human development and democracy. He was highly critical of the extreme inequalities of income, wealth, and power, which hindered the human development of the lower classes. Mill's ideas of participation and equality create a tension in his work because they are hard to reconcile with his positions concerning a restricted government committed to laissez-faire (which can be interpreted as doing nothing about the inequalities) and a plural voting system in favor of the well-educated (which is hardly a radical commitment to equality).[15]

Several other thinkers have shared Mill's preoccupation with participation as an important element of democracy and his concern that socioeconomic inequality is a main barrier to democracy and political equality. An early contribution in this respect was made by Jean-Jacques Rousseau (1712–1778) almost a hundred years before J. S. Mill. Rousseau's point of departure was a small, preindustrial community. He criticized the notion of representation, saying that citizens should be directly involved in the making of their laws; otherwise, there is no freedom. "The English people believes itself to be free, it is gravely mistaken; it is free only during the election of Members of Parliament; as soon as the members are elected, the people are enslaved; it is nothing."[16] In other words, real freedom calls for participation in the form of direct democracy.

Rousseau's ideas about the role of participation in democracy have often been rejected because they are seen as irrelevant for modern, large-scale society. But in more recent contributions, C. B. Macpherson and Carol Pateman have argued that Rousseau's ideas are indeed compatible with modern society and that representative government can be combined with elements of direct participation and indeed ought to be if democracy is to be more than merely formal.[17] According to Macpherson and Pateman, structures of participation in local society and in the workplace will vastly improve the quality of representative democracy. A participatory society would make the common man "better able to assess the performance of representatives at the national level, better equipped to take decisions of national scope when the opportunity arose to do so, and better able to weigh up the impact of decisions taken by national representatives on his own life."[18]

Like J. S. Mill, Rousseau felt that socioeconomic inequality would prevent citizens from equal political rights. In other words, with vast socioeconomic inequalities there could be no political democracy. In his critical analysis of capitalism, Karl Marx (1818–1883) related the existence of inequality with the class division produced by capitalist society itself. In Marx's view, in a capitalist society a free market and a state based on politically equal citizens are simply formalities that hide the reality of rule by the capitalist class. The only way to achieve real political and economic equality and a full democratization of state and society is to abolish the capitalist system and replace it with socialism and ultimately communism.[19] Thus, Marx agreed with Hayek that there is a sharp distinction between liberalism and democracy, but he drew the opposite conclusion: In order to achieve liberty and democracy, it is necessary to reject liberal capitalism.

In the debate about the relationship between capitalism and democracy, the liberalist tradition maintains that only a capitalist system can provide the necessary basis for liberty and democracy. The Marxist tradition finds that capitalism must be replaced by socialism as the necessary basis for democracy. The liberal view has prevailed insofar as the noncapitalist countries that have declared adherence to the Marxist tradition have been unable to construct political systems that can claim to be more democratic than the liberal democracies based on capitalism.

Yet the debate does not end there. Far from all of the capitalist systems in the world are also democratic. And it should be stressed that one does not have to be a Marxist in order to see the obstacles to democracy stemming from economic inequality. In a recent contribution, Robert Dahl stated that modern corporate capitalism tends to "produce inequalities in social and economic resources so great as to bring about severe violations of political equality and hence of the democratic process."[20] Dahl went on to suggest a system of cooperative control over the economy. This view of the need to extend democratic decision-making beyond government, to economic and social life as well, is also expressed in other recent contributions.[21]

Thus, the current debate about capitalism and democracy is not greatly concerned about the abolition of capitalism; the debate is between such thinkers as Hayek, on the one side, who wanted to protect life, liberty, and estate by rolling back government intervention in civil society, and a liberal cum social democratic group, on the other side, that argues for the necessity of a more reformed capitalism with less inequality and more democracy, not only in strictly political affairs but also in social and economic life.[22]

THE MEANING OF DEMOCRACY

It is clear from this brief overview of important debates concerning democracy that the questions asked at the beginning of this chapter about the meaning of rule by the people involve so many complex elements that they are far from easily answered. Indeed, a full answer to the question of what democracy means today requires a theory of contemporary society supported by substantial normative considerations about the type of people's rule that is desirable, which cannot be pursued here. Instead, I will illustrate the scope of this debate by outlining two conceptions of democracy with contemporary relevance: one rather narrow, the other very comprehensive. From each side, they help delimit the territory within which the debate about democracy has taken place.

The narrow concept was formulated by Joseph Schumpeter. For him democracy was simply a political method, a mechanism for choosing political leadership. The citizens are given a choice among rival political leaders who compete for their votes. Between elections, decisions are made by the politicians. At the next election, citizens can replace their elected officials. This ability to choose between leaders at election time is democracy. In Schumpeter's words, "The democratic method is that institutional arrangement for arriving at political decisions in which individuals acquire the power to decide by means of a competitive struggle for the people's vote."[23]

At the opposite end of the spectrum we have the very comprehensive notion of democracy suggested by David Held. Held combined insights of the liberal and the Marxist traditions in order to arrive at a meaning of democracy that supports a basic principle of autonomy:

> Individuals should be free and equal in the determination of the conditions of their own lives; that is, they should enjoy equal rights (and, accordingly, equal obligations) in the specification of the framework which generates and limits the opportunities available to them, so long as they do not deploy this framework to negate the rights of others.[24]

The enactment of this principle, which Held called **democratic autonomy,** requires both a high degree of accountability of the state and a democratic reordering of civil society. It foresees substantial direct participation in local community institutions as well as self-management of cooperatively owned enterprises. It calls for a bill of rights that goes beyond the right to cast a vote to include equal opportunity for participation and for discovering individual preferences as well as citizens' final control of the political agenda. Also included are social and economic rights to ensure adequate resources for democratic autonomy. "Without tough social and economic rights, rights with respect to the state could not be fully enjoyed; and without state rights new forms of inequality of power, wealth and status could systematically disrupt the implementation of social and economic liberties."[25]

In the area between the narrow notion of political democracy suggested by Schumpeter and the extremely comprehensive understanding presented by Held lies the debate about what democracy is and what it ought to be. Looking at democracy this way helps us understand that it is a dynamic entity that has been given many different definitions; its meaning remains subject to debate.

This approach can also help us see the possibility of emphasizing different aspects of democracy in framing one's own understanding of the concept. It is not surprising, for example, that conditions in many developing countries have led to an emphasis on the need to meet basic economic rights and equal opportunities for participation, as stressed in Held's comprehensive notion of democracy. Extreme material poverty makes democracy difficult:

> Where the members of a community suffer from chronic malnutrition and frequent illness, participation in common affairs that is both broad and deep

is difficult to maintain. Where the lot of the masses is often that of acute hunger, or where disease runs rampant, the expectation of any genuine democracy among such masses is naive.[26]

It is against such a background that Julius Nyerere, the former president of Tanzania, said that the struggle for freedom in Africa is basically a struggle for freedom from hunger, disease, and poverty.

In the industrialized countries, where extreme poverty is not the main problem, there can be other impediments to democracy—for example, the lack of economic, social, and, consequently, political equality stressed by Dahl. At the same time, many of us would agree that the Western industrialized countries are, in a basic respect, democracies, particularly according to the narrow concept of political democracy provided by Schumpeter.

One general conclusion that can be drawn from this discussion of the meaning of democracy is that there can be no talk of the "**end of history**"[27] even if the authoritarian, noncapitalist regimes of the East have collapsed. (The end of history is a phrase coined by Francis Fukuyama to describe the end point of humankind's ideological evolution and the universalization of Western liberal democracy as the final form of human government.) There is still plenty of room for the development of different variations or models of democracy.

*   *   *

In another respect this view of the meaning of democracy is less helpful. It does not give us much guidance in determining whether specific countries are democratic. For that purpose we need a precise concept that provides a clear identification of what democracy essentially is. It is necessary, in other words, to cut through the debates in order to find a tool with which we can identify democracy by its core features, as a form of government in which the people rule. Most helpful would be a narrow concept that focuses on democracy as a specific type of political system. In the very broad concept, democracy is not only a political but also a specific social and economic system. In other words, if we were to use the broad concept we would be able to find very few, if indeed any, empirical cases of democracy. Furthermore, when democracy is seen in a narrow sense as a political system, it is easier to ask questions about the relationships between this political system, on the one hand, and the economic and social dimensions, on the other. It must be emphasized that although the narrow concept of democracy provides the most adequate starting point for the analysis intended here, it is not a normative choice of the "best kind" of democracy.

A contribution by Robert A. Dahl is helpful in defining democracy as a political system. Dahl emphasized the responsiveness of the government to the preferences of its citizens, considered as political equals, as a key characteristic of democracy. Such responsiveness requires that citizens must have opportunities to (1) formulate their preferences, (2) signify their preferences to their fellow citizens and the government by individual and collective action, and (3) have their preferences weighed equally in the conduct of the government. These three opportunities, in turn, are dependent on the following institutional guarantees:

1. Freedom to form and join organizations
2. Freedom of expression
3. Right to vote
4. Eligibility for public office
5. Right of political leaders to compete for support
   5a. Right of political leaders to compete for votes
6. Alternative sources of information
7. Free and fair elections
8. Institutions for making government policies depend on votes and other expressions of preference[28]

When these conditions are met, we have a political democracy. It is sometimes referred to as a liberal democracy because of its focus on the form of government. Dahl noted that there is no country in which these conditions are perfectly satisfied; he therefore prefers the term **polyarchy** for concrete systems and reserves the democracy label for the nonexistent, ideal type. In this book the term democracy or political democracy will be used for the systems Dahl would call polyarchies.

In principle, the eight conditions outlined by Dahl make up our definition of political democracy. Yet for practical purposes it will be helpful to come up with an even more condensed definition that summarizes the basic elements of political democracy. The eight conditions cover three main dimensions of political democracy, namely *competition, participation,* and *civil and political liberties.*[29] Against this background, political democracy can be viewed as a system of government that meets the following conditions:

- Meaningful and extensive *competition* among individuals and organized groups (especially political parties) for all effective positions of government power, at regular intervals and excluding the use of force
- A highly inclusive level of *political participation* in the selection of leaders and policies, at least through regular and fair elections, such that no major (adult) social group is excluded

- A level of *civil and political liberties*—freedom of expression, freedom of the press, freedom to form and join organizations—sufficient to ensure the integrity of political competition and participation[30]

This is the definition of political democracy that is to be employed in the present volume.

Our first task in attempting to determine whether a specific country is a democracy is to look for the presence of the elements of competition, participation, and liberties in that country, not just on the formal level but in real practice. (There are many examples of political leaders who pay lip service to democratic ideals without meeting them in practice.) This task is complicated by the fact that many countries meet the conditions specified by the three dimensions in varying degrees.

Thus, it is necessary to decide on some minimum value that should be met with regard to each dimension for a country to qualify as democratic. For those that do not qualify, further differentiation is necessary because they vary substantially in their degrees of nondemocracy. For example, Mexico may not have been fully democratic in the postwar period, but it has been much more democratic than Chile has been under the Pinochet dictatorship. Differentiating degrees of nondemocracy is another substantial task; in the area between full democracy and nondemocracy (or authoritarian rule), there is room for highly different types of semi-democracies and semi-authoritarian systems.[31]

Unfortunately, there is no agreement among scholars about which of the dimensions are most important in determining whether there is democracy or about what precise minimum value should be applied for each of the dimensions. Moreover, just trying to analyze the particular conditions specified by the three dimensions can often be difficult (e.g., was an election rigged; do opposition parties get fair possibilities for competing?).

We shall return to attempts to measure political democracy in a moment. It is helpful first to look briefly at processes of democratization based on the concept of democracy we have just outlined and to indicate the relationship between political democracy as competition, participation, and liberties and the very broad concept of democracy formulated by Held.

When democracy is defined in terms of competition, participation, and liberties, it is clear that the process of democratization, the change of a political system from nondemocratic toward more democratic, can take place in different ways. Dahl identified two principal routes toward democracy: one with a focus on competition, the other with a focus on participation.[32] Increased participation (or **inclusiveness**) means that the proportion of citizens who enjoy political rights and liberties increases. Nondemocratic regimes may exclude a large majority of the population from participation. In democratic regimes the entire adult population enjoys the full range of rights and liberties.

Competition (or **liberalization**) concerns the extent to which rights and liberties are available to at least some members of the political system. Increasing liberalization means increasing the possibility for political opposition and competition for government power. Figure 1.1 illustrates possible paths from nondemocratic rule toward democracy, each involving a different degree of participation and competition.

Four countries are mentioned in the figure. Denmark is an example of a democracy in which the entire adult population enjoys the full range of rights and liberties. In the former USSR, elections were regularly held and all adults had the right to vote, but opposition to the ruling Communist party was not possible. In other words, there was a high degree of participation but there was no political competition and there were no real liberties, such as freedom of expression, the right to form organizations, and access to alternative sources of information. Therefore, the USSR was not a democracy. The present process of democratization in the former USSR is first and foremost a process of liberalization, of increased political competition backed by real rights and liberties. In South Africa, the situation is different. For many years, a white minority has enjoyed the political rights and liberties necessary for political competition, whereas the black majority has been excluded from participation. In this case, the process of democratization is primarily one of increasing participation through the inclusion of the black population. Finally, the dictatorship in Chile under Augusto Pinochet has offered neither competition nor participation to any parts of the population. Since 1988, Chile has undergone a process of democratization that has increased both liberalization and participation, but it has not yet made the full transition to democracy. The processes of democratization will be subject to further scrutiny in Chapter 2, where additional concrete examples of different paths toward democracy will be given.

How does the comprehensive notion of democracy outlined by Held fit into this picture? Held's concept of democracy can be seen as an expansion of political democracy in two respects: further liberalization and more participation. In other words, having reached political democracy, further democratization is still possible according to the broad concept of democracy set forth by Held. On one dimension, this means additional liberalization: Formal political rights and liberties may be worth little if citizens are not secured equal rights in a more substantial manner. For example, without a welfare state that prevents extreme material poverty and steep socioeconomic inequalities, it is not possible for the poor sec-

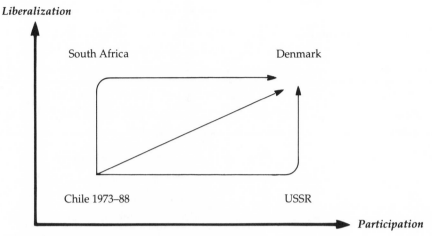

FIGURE 1.1 Dimensions of democratization

Source: Modified from Robert A. Dahl, *Polyarchy: Participation and Opposition* (New Haven: Yale University Press, 1971), p. 7, and Palle Svensson, "The Liberalization of Eastern Europe," *Journal of Behavioral and Social Sciences* 34 (1991): 56.

tions of the population to fully enjoy their political rights. Only with poverty eradicated can formally equal rights be translated into substantially equal rights.

It is also possible to extend the other dimension, participation. According to our definition of political democracy, participation concerns government and public institutions. In Held's notion of democracy, participation is extended to social institutions and the economy (note his suggestions about the self-management of enterprises and participation in local community institutions). The movement from political democracy toward Held's notion of democratic autonomy is summarized in Figure 1.2.

The figure demonstrates how the combination of extended liberalization and participation defines the movement from political democracy toward democratic autonomy. It must be stressed that focus in this volume is *not* on the processes going beyond political democracy. The focus is on the processes of democratization depicted in Figure 1.1—that is, the movement from authoritarian rule toward political democracy. Therefore, the terms democracy and political democracy will be used interchangeably.

We now have (1) a definition of political democracy as participation, competition, and civil and political liberties; (2) a notion of paths of democratization; and (3) a sense of the relationship between political democracy and the much broader concept of democratic autonomy. The following section looks at attempts to measure democracy, using our definition of political democracy as the starting point.

FIGURE 1.2   The movement from political democracy toward democratic autonomy

Source: Modified from Guillermo O'Donnell and Philippe C. Schmitter, *Transitions from Authoritarian Rule: Tentative Conclusions About Uncertain Democracies* (Baltimore: Johns Hopkins University Press, 1986), p. 13.

ATTEMPTS TO MEASURE DEMOCRACY

With the difficulties it involves, it is no surprise that the measurement of democracy has become its own branch of political science surrounded by an ongoing debate about best ways of devising and combining indicators. Because of the large number of difficulties in this domain, one should treat attempts at estimating the quantity of democracy with caution. The indexes and overviews are helpful as starting points, but a closer inspection of countries must follow.

The most recent attempt to measure the degree of democracy in a large number of countries using Dahl's concept of democracy as a starting point was undertaken by Tatu Vanhanen.[33] Unfortunately, his study, which covers the years 1980 to 1988, does not provide data about the most recent transitions toward democracy. Therefore, I shall rely on another well-known attempt at measuring democracy, namely the Freedom House index.[34]

The index employs one dimension for competition and participation (called political rights) and one dimension for civil liberties. For each dimension a seven-point scale is used, so that the highest ranking countries (that is, those with the highest degree of democracy) are one-ones (1–1's) and the lowest are seven-sevens (7–7's). In other words, the index attempts to reflect the space of semi-democracy or semi-authoritarianism between outright authoritarian (7–7) and fully democratic (1–1) regimes (see Fig. 1.3).

Countries with an average rating between 1 and 2.5 are considered free; those with an average between 3 and 5.5 are partly free; and those with

Classification of Countries	Political rights Rating 1–7	Civil liberties Rating 1–7
	Combined average ranking	
Free	1–2.5	
Partly Free	3–5.5	
Not free	5.5–7	

FIGURE 1.3   The Freedom House index for measuring democracy. Note that countries with a 5.5 average are classified as either partly free or not free depending on which raw scores the overall ranking summarizes.

Source: Based on R. Bruce McColm, "The Comparative Survey of Freedom: 1991," *Freedom Review* 22, no. 1 (1991): 14.

ratings from 5.5 to 7 are considered not free. Although the Freedom House distinction between rights and liberties differs from the breakdown of components in the definition of democracy we are employing, both basically cover the same dimensions. Therefore, the Freedom House index can function as an approximate measurement of political democracy as defined in this book.

The 1996–1997 Freedom House survey of independent countries with more than one million inhabitants identified forty-nine countries as free. The list, shown in Table 1.1, is ordered according to combined average ratings. When countries with fewer than one million inhabitants were included (bringing the total number of states in the world to 191), the Freedom House survey for 1996–1997 classified seventy-nine countries as free, fifty-nine as partly free, and another fifty-three as not free.[35]

Two caveats are worth stressing in relation to the Freedom House survey and other indexes. First, they provide only rough approximations of the possible presence and status of democracy in a country. They are incapable of revealing many of the features of political systems. For example, the features that made one scholar characterize Japan as soft authoritarian do not come clearly forward in any of these indexes. Chalmers Johnson presented the following argument:

> Since 1947, despite its adoption of a formally democratic constitution and the subsequent development of a genuinely open political culture, Japan seems to have retained many "**soft authoritarian**" features in its governmental institutions: an extremely strong and comparatively unsupervised state administration, single-party rule for more than three decades, and a set of economic priorities that seems unattainable under true political pluralism during such a long period.[36]

TABLE 1.1   The Freedom House Index Classification of Free Countries (with greater than one million inhabitants), 1997

Average rating: 1

Australia	Ireland	Sweden
Austria	Netherlands	Switzerland
Canada	New Zealand	United States
Denmark	Norway	
Finland	Portugal	

Average rating: 1.5

Belgium	Hungary	Slovenia
Costa Rica	Italy	South Africa
Czech Republic	Japan	Spain
Estonia	Lithuania	United Kingdom
France	Mauritius	Uruguay
Germany	Poland	

Average rating: 2

Benin	Greece	Latvia
Botswana	Israel	Taiwan
Chile	Korea, South	

Average rating: 2.5

Argentina	Malawi	Philippines
Bolivia	Mongolia	Romania
Bulgaria	Namibia	Venezuela
Jamaica	Panama	

Source: Based on data from *Freedom Review* 28, no. 1 (1997): 15.

Indeed, Japan may be superficially characterized as a parliamentary democracy, but its political system is profoundly different from the Western system, with power in Japan vested in institutions to which there are no clear parallels in the West.[37] Other commentators have been even harsher in their criticism of what they see as the lack of real democracy in Japan, but the political rights and political liberties dimensions employed by Freedom House do not reveal such problems.[38]

Thus, actual cases of democracy are often highly dissimilar in important dimensions. We may include such systems as those of the United States, Botswana, Denmark, Costa Rica, Japan, and Jamaica under the general term democracies, but the specific structures of their political systems, their political culture, and their socioeconomic environments are substantially different. One scholar has suggested making the following distinctions between various types of democratic regimes: presidential versus parliamentary; majoritarian versus representational; two-party versus multiparty; distribution of power among parties; extremist multiparty; and consociational. He defined a **consociational democracy** as one that has mechanisms serving to promote compromise and consensus among groups in society.[39]

Therefore, detailed analysis of specific cases is necessary in order to ascertain in a more profound manner their democratic qualities. It is only at the level of the individual case that one can study the interplay between formal freedoms, political processes, and the larger context of socioeconomic and other conditions that affect the quality of democracy. Furthermore, if we agree with Held that democracy is made much more difficult by extreme material poverty, then it also becomes relevant to look at socioeconomic conditions as co-determinants of the quality of democracy, even if these conditions are not included in the definition of democracy as a political system. The Human Development index compiled by the United Nations Development Programme (UNDP) provides systematic, comparative information on these conditions.[40]

In countries like Benin or Malawi, where large parts of the adult population are illiterate and a substantial number of people live below the poverty line, a vigorous democracy is more difficult to achieve than in countries with better socioeconomic conditions. This observation is also relevant for many other African countries, where the situation is similar or even worse, and for such countries as Bolivia, Mongolia, Jamaica, and the Philippines.

Some scholars draw the dramatic conclusion that it is impossible to have democracy in any meaningful sense in materially very poor societies.[41] That might be going too far. Socioeconomic conditions do affect the *quality* of political democracy but they do not prevent the development of a democratic system.

At the same time, it is necessary to be aware that socioeconomic inequalities can impede real political equality in industrialized countries as well. Some data on socioeconomic conditions in industrialized countries can also be found in the UNDP report.[42]

The second caveat that should be stressed with regard to the indexes that estimate degrees of democracy concerns the "new" democracies, which will be analyzed in further detail in the next chapter. These democracies are in the early stages of what might be a long process of transition from authoritarian toward democratic rule. In other words, the ratings these new democracies receive in the indexes are really only snapshots of regimes that are "on the move"—that is, in a process of transition from one form of regime toward another.

TIME HORIZONS AND LEVELS OF ANALYSIS

It is useful to introduce two additional elements in this general presentation of the meaning and prevalence of democracy. The first is the historical dimension. One must remember that in historical terms, democracy as

it has been defined here is a very recent phenomenon. Only four countries—Australia, Finland, New Zealand, and Norway—had extended suffrage to women before World War I. And even if we look for "male
democracies" in existence then, we would not find many cases; the constitutional monarchies in nineteenth-century Europe cannot be considered
fully democratic because their cabinets were not responsible to elected
Parliaments in a clear-cut manner.[43]

Thus, the semi-democracies of nineteenth-century Europe became fully
democratic only in the twentieth century, and several of them, including
Italy, Germany, Austria, and Spain, suffered setbacks to nondemocratic
rule in the 1920s and 1930s. Consequently, it is only for the period after
World War II that one can talk about extended, stable democratic rule in
the industrialized countries of Western Europe and North America.

In the developing countries of Asia, Africa, and Latin America, there
have been only a handful of enduring democracies, among them Costa
Rica, India, Venezuela (from 1958), and Jamaica (from 1962). In recent
years, transitions toward more democratic rule have taken place in a large
number of developing countries and countries of Eastern Europe. The
question must be asked whether this phenomenon is a prelude to an era
of many more stable democracies than we have seen so far or is merely a
fragile flourish that can easily suffer setbacks to nondemocracy. This issue
will be addressed in Chapter 2.

The other dimension that must be introduced here concerns levels of
analysis. Until now, our discussion about what democracy is and where it
can be found has focused on the state: Does this or that country have
democracy or not? But this level of analysis is clearly insufficient. There is
an international or global level "above" the states and a local level "below" them that must also be taken into account.

How does the *international system* affect prospects for democracy in individual countries? To answer this question, one must analyze the dominant trends in the international system and the different ways in which
they affect specific countries. It is probably universally agreed that during
the postwar period there has been an enormous increase in all types of exchange between countries, including trade, investment, communication,
and travel. In other words, there is a higher degree of **interdependence**
(situations characterized by mutual dependence between countries or
among actors in different countries) than ever before.[44]

Against this background, ideas about democracy and human rights
have been increasingly diffused. Russian Nobel laureate Andrei Sakharov
called the United Nations declaration of human rights the common glue
that binds all ideologies together, and state leaders have felt a growing
need to appeal to democratic ideas in order to legitimize their rule. There
is no doubt that the Helsinki factor—the pressure from the West for more
respect for basic human rights in Eastern Europe and the former Soviet

Union—has played an important part in the democratic openings there, as we shall see in Chapter 2. Yet leading Western countries such as the United States, France, and Great Britain have not provided consistent support for the promotion of democracy in all parts of the world. They have, on several occasions, supported nondemocratic leaders in Asia, Africa, and Latin America for reasons of national interest.

At the same time, individual countries are to an increasing degree being subjected to international forces over which they have little control. It is true, as Dahl pointed out, that this has always been the case: "Not just conflict but also trade, commerce, and finance have always spilled over state boundaries. Democratic states, therefore, have never been able to act autonomously, in disregard of the actions of outside forces over which they had little or no control."[45] But recent tendencies are more than just replays of this theme. In developing countries, for example, dependence on international structures has increased in the wake of the debt crisis, which has expanded the power over single countries of such international organizations as the International Monetary Fund (IMF) and the World Bank. The frustration of these countries to this increased dependency came out clearly in a speech by Julius Nyerere of Tanzania in 1979: "When did the IMF become an International Ministry of Finance? When did nations agree to surrender their power of decision making?"[46] The IMF response to questions such as these would probably be that the fund acts only on the basis of agreements entered by countries on a voluntary basis.

No clear conclusion emerges from these brief remarks on the effects of the international system on democracy in single countries. I shall return to the issue in the coming chapters. What we may note for now is that actors in the international system can either promote or try to prevent democracy in single countries. Moreover, the dynamics of dependence and interdependence in the international system directly affect the scope of democratic decision-making at the national level. In general, one must expect large and socioeconomically strong countries to be much less susceptible to international pressures and challenges than is the case with smaller, socioeconomically weak countries.

Let me turn to the *local level* of analysis. Until now we have assumed that democracy at the level of national government in a country means that democracy also prevails at the local level. Yet this need not always be the case. Examples from India and China illustrate this point.

India is one of the few countries in the Third World with a long democratic tradition. It adopted a democratic constitution in 1950, and for only eighteen months, in 1975–1977, during the so-called emergency declared by Indira Gandhi, was there nondemocratic rule. However, democracy at the national or macro level of the political system has not meant that democracy was brought to all localities. The Congress party attained its dominant position in India's vast countryside by making alliances that enforced the traditional patterns of domination. Congress dealt with the electorate through "existing patron-brokers who, as landowners and caste-leaders, had no desire to jeopardize their positions by transforming local social structures. In adapting to local conditions, the party thus increasingly became tied to age-old patterns of status and leadership."[47] Against this background, it is not surprising that democratic India has set in motion programs that, although claiming to promote welfare and participation at the local level, have in fact had the opposite effect: making the poor majority even worse off and strengthening the traditional structures of dominance and subordination.[48] In the 1990s, more intense communal violence, especially between militant Hindus and Muslims, has meant some setback for democracy; the current classification of India by Freedom House is 4-4 (1997).

In China, political democracy like that found in India was never seriously on the agenda. The Chinese Communist party (CCP) is a Bolshevik party; it did not propose to fight for the interests of all Chinese but only for the interests of workers and poor peasants against internal and external class enemies. Further, the democracy it sought for workers and poor peasants was the democracy of leadership from above combined with some degree of participation from below, and it gave special status to the small faction of the population (less than 1 percent in 1949) who were members of the party.[49]

But it can be claimed that the Communists, within this overall structure of authoritarian socialist rule, also promoted at least some elements of democracy at the local level. They did so through what was called the mass line, which took at least five different forms.[50] First, grass-roots and county-level leaders were given a high degree of latitude in ensuring that higher-level instructions were in accordance with local needs, conditions, and opinions. Second, cadres were sent to the villages to work and live alongside the peasants, under similar circumstances, in order to share their experiences and learn from rural life. Third, secret ballot elections were held regularly at village, township, county, and regional levels, providing a democratic and representative character to local government. "The only restriction was the 'three-thirds' principle, according to which one-third of offices were to be filled by CCP members, one-third by non-CCP leftists, and one-third by liberals."[51] Fourth, popular political expression in the form of the "big character poster" (dazibao, or wall poster) was encouraged. And, finally, the armed forces were to take part in civilian affairs under rules that required their subordination to civil authority.

The difference between China and India at the local level is quite clear: The authoritarian Chinese government has pushed structural reforms and systems of local participation that have done more for democratic change at the micro level than the so-called reforms attempted by democratic India. I am not suggesting that this contradiction between democracy (or nondemocracy) at the national level and nondemocratic tendencies (or the opposite) at the local level can be widely generalized. The core of the matter is that a national framework of democracy does not guarantee real democracy at the local level and an authoritarian national framework does not completely block democratic elements at the local level.

Yet one can expect such contradictions to become less pronounced in the long run. In other words, in the long run, democracy at the national level and democracy at the local level tend to reinforce each other, but in the short-to-medium run there may be discrepancies between the two. It is important to be aware of these discrepancies in overall assessments of democracy.

CONCLUSION

Democracy means rule by the people. A more precise definition is difficult to formulate because democracy is a dynamic entity that has acquired many different meanings over the course of time. Much of this dynamic comes from changes in society and from the different interpretations by analysts of the consequences of these changes for democracy. With the very different levels and ways of development of societies in today's world, it is not surprising that the meaning of democracy continues to be the subject of debate.

Yet for analytical purposes we need to develop a concept that provides a clear identification of what democracy essentially is. The core of political democracy has three dimensions: competition, participation, and civil and political liberties. When we study the status of democracy in a specific country, the first step is to look for these three elements. In this context it is helpful to consult one of the indexes on democracy—for example, the Freedom House index. In order to make a comprehensive assessment of democracy, one must carefully scrutinize the individual country as well because democratic systems vary greatly in their institutional patterns and along other dimensions. Socioeconomic conditions also affect the quality of democracy. Finally, it is necessary to be aware of the international setting above and the local conditions below the level of national government.

It can be argued that this procedure is too comprehensive and requires analysis of "everything." It is true that one will often have to stop short of completing all of these stages. Even in the present volume the discussion is limited to the transition from authoritarian rule to political democracy and to the consequences of democracy. Yet it is important to be aware of the full agenda if one wishes to evaluate specific cases of democracy in a more comprehensive manner.

TWO

□ □ □

Processes
of Democratization

What conditions are conducive to the formation of a political democracy? The first two sections of this chapter introduce the debate about the effects of general economic, social, and other conditions on the rise of democracy. Some conditions favor democracy more than others, but it will be argued that for a full understanding one must study the interplay between these conditions, on the one hand, and the choices made by political actors, on the other.

And why have such a large number of countries begun the transition toward democracy in recent years? A model of the process of democratization will be introduced that demonstrates that the movement from authoritarian to democratic rule is a complex, long-term process involving different phases; the current transitions are only in the beginning of this process. The bulk of this chapter is devoted to the formulation of four propositions, each of which spells out an important characteristic of the current transitions. The propositions serve to substantiate the dilemma identified in the introduction: Democracy has made progress in terms of democratic openings, but it has progressed in a way that does not bode well for further democratic consolidation. The result may just as easily be a democratic deadlock in which frail and unconsolidated democracies fail to meet the hopes and promises invested in them by the majorities of the populations.

THE SEARCH FOR DEMOCRACY'S PRECONDITIONS

What pattern of economic, social, cultural, and other conditions is most favorable to the rise of democracy? It was noted in Chapter 1 that the spread of democracy is a relatively recent phenomenon. The implication seems to be that it takes the conditions brought about by modern, indus-

24

trial society to produce democracy. This idea was behind the famous thesis by Seymour M. Lipset: "The more well-to-do a nation, the greater the chances that it will sustain democracy."[1]

Modernization and wealth will always be accompanied by a number of factors conducive to democracy: higher rates of literacy and education, urbanization, the development of mass media. Moreover, wealth will also provide the resources needed to mitigate the tensions produced by political conflict.[2] A large number of empirical analyses inspired by the Lipset hypothesis tended to support it. Thus, in 1971 Robert Dahl considered it "pretty much beyond dispute" that the higher the socioeconomic level of a country, the more likely that it would be a democracy.[3]

But this expectation far from always holds true. Argentina has had many years of authoritarian rule despite a relatively high level of per capita income; the same can be said of Taiwan and South Korea. In the latter cases, rapid economic development has even been accompanied by a fairly equal distribution of income. In his analysis of the major South American cases, Guillermo O'Donnell developed an argument that turned the Lipset thesis on its head: Authoritarianism, not democracy, seemed to him to be the more likely concomitant of the highest levels of modernization. O'Donnell's reasoning went as follows: The process of industrial modernization that was taking place in several Latin American countries in the 1960s and early 1970s had very little to offer the large majority of the populations. Therefore, in order to pursue this model in the face of popular resistance, the ruling elite needs an authoritarian system.[4]

A second set of preconditions (the first set being associated with modernization and wealth) often brought forward in the attempt to determine the factors that favor democracy concerns **political culture**—that is, the system of values and beliefs that defines the context and meaning of political action. If political culture is tied in with the larger system of culture in a society, is it possible to identify cultural values and beliefs that are especially conducive to democracy?

One of the frequent answers to this question is that Protestantism supports democracy whereas Catholicism in many cases, especially in Latin America, works against it. In more general terms, some cultures emphasize hierarchy, authority, and intolerance more than others. It seems reasonable to expect that they are less conducive to democracy. Islam and Confucianism are like Catholicism in this regard.

Yet it is difficult to demonstrate a systematic relationship between specific cultural patterns and the prevalence of democracy.[5] Moreover, cultural systems are subject to dynamic change. It may be that Catholicism did, at one point in history, work against democracy in Latin America, but the Catholic church also played an active role in the opposition toward authoritarian rule in the 1980s.[6]

A third set of preconditions favoring democracy is associated with the social structure of society, that is, the specific classes and groups making up the society. Is it possible to identify certain groups and classes that consistently favor democracy (for example, the middle classes, industrial bourgeoisie, workers) and others that consistently work against it (for example, traditional landowners)?

In his historical account of the roots of democracy and dictatorship, Barrington Moore concluded that "a vigorous and independent class of town dwellers has been an indispensable element in the growth of parliamentary democracy. No bourgeois, no democracy."[7] Conversely, landowners tend to support democracy only under special circumstances, such as when small-scale farming is dominant and there is a relatively equal distribution of land. Against Barrington Moore's thesis it must be said that the bourgeoisie does not consistently work for democracy. It has in fact been argued that the opposite is closer to the truth. According to Goran Therborn, democracy has "always and everywhere" been brought about in a popular struggle against the leading sections of the bourgeoisie.[8]

The final set of possible preconditions to be mentioned here is made up of **external factors,** the economic, political, ideological, and other elements that constitute the international context for the processes that take place in single countries. It was argued in Chapter 1 that no straightforward conclusion is possible regarding the effect of external factors on democracy. The developing countries of the Third World are those most susceptible to external influence, especially by the leading Western countries. It is customary among modernization theorists to consider this influence beneficial for the promotion of democracy.[9] Dependency theorists have drawn the opposite conclusion: The inequalities and distortions of the economies and societies of the Third World, brought about by their dependent position in the world economic system, make democracy very difficult.[10]

Four sets of possible preconditions for democracy have now been identified. It is possible to continue the list, of course. Dahl named seventeen variables, classified into seven categories, that are conducive to democracy.[11] Larry Diamond, Juan Linz, and Seymour Lipset employed a similar procedure in the introduction to their study of democracy in developing countries.[12] Yet for every factor seen as conducive to democracy, counterexamples can be put forward. Moreover, in many countries, different preconditions may exist that point in different directions: For example, cultural factors may be conducive to democracy while economic factors may not be.

The situation is somewhat frustrating. It is possible to point out a number of preconditions that can reasonably be expected to favor or obstruct the possibilities for democracy. But in every case it is also possible to give counterexamples, where the expectations have not held true.

Thus, a fixed model or law about democracy cannot be formulated. We cannot say that if x, y, or n preconditions are present, there will be democracy. In one sense, it is fortunate that a law of this kind is infeasible. For it would leave little or no room for the choices taken by political actors. Such choices make a difference. Juan Linz has noted that in some situations "even the presence of an individual with unique qualities and characteristics—a Charles de Gaulle, for instance—can be decisive and cannot be predicted by any model."[13] In a similar way, many observers give credit to Nelson Mandela for his essential role in South Africa's transition to democracy.

In some cases, as we shall see, democracy can emerge even when none, or very few, of the preconditions listed as conducive to democracy are present. Economic, social, cultural, and other structural conditions may well act as constraints decreasing the likelihood for democracy to occur, but they do not themselves make the policy choice about whether there will be a democratic system.

However, recognizing the importance of choices taken by political actors does not mean that the search for preconditions is completely useless. Actors cannot make any kind of choice in a given situation. They are constrained by the structures—the preconditions—that are the result of the country's development in previous periods. Therefore, one must look at the interplay between economic, social, cultural, and other preconditions created in earlier periods and the decisions taken by current political actors.

The preconditions set the stage; they form the scene on which the actors play.[14] The preconditions cannot foretell whether the actors will produce democracy or not, but they can provide some information about what kind of outcome we can expect from the players. For example, even if democracy does not always occur under high levels of economic development, a country's democratic prospects are better at higher rather than lower levels of economic development. Although very poor countries with adverse social, economic, and other preconditions may well move toward democracy (as can be seen currently in some African countries), we can expect that outcome to be much more rare than in countries with more favorable preconditions. We must also expect the democracies emerging under such adverse conditions to be highly unstable, frail, and vulnerable. In sum, although the search for economic, cultural, social, institutional, and other preconditions may not yield any law-like results, they do give us important information about the prospects for democracy.

In the final analysis, there is no way around a more detailed study of the interplay of actors and structures in concrete settings. Before we move in that direction, however, it is useful to discuss in more general terms the choices made by political actors.

WHEN DO POLITICAL ACTORS CHOOSE DEMOCRACY?

Democracy does not fall from heaven. It is brought about by individuals and groups, by social actors, who fight for it. Adam Przeworski has made a penetrating analysis of the choices taken by the important actors in moving their countries toward democracy.[15] His starting point was the contention that democracy basically introduces a degree of uncertainty in the political process. In a democracy, no single group can be sure that its interests will ultimately prevail. Even the most powerful group, be it local or foreign business, armed forces, bureaucracy, or other privileged elements, must be ready to face the possibility that it can lose out in conflicts with other groups, which means that its interests may not be looked after. In other words, in democracies actors may choose policy reforms that attack the power and privilege of dominant groups.

Given this situation, it is not difficult to see why the nonprivileged, who were barred from political influence during authoritarian rule, struggle for a democratic polity that will give them access to political influence. But why should members of the dominant forces, who held together in the power bloc behind nondemocratic, authoritarian rule, suddenly opt for a democratic solution that may entail a threat to their interests?

They may try to avoid the democratic option, of course. That is, they may strive to keep the authoritarian system. Insofar as there is regime change, it is merely from one type of authoritarian regime to another. Alternatively, democracy may prevail, even against the wishes of the dominant forces, because the authoritarian regime suffers defeat in a foreign or a civil war or simply disintegrates due to internal division.[16]

However, transitions to democracy are only very rarely based on the complete defeat of the elites who stood behind the previous authoritarian rule. In the vast majority of cases the transition to democracy is based on negotiations with the forces backing the authoritarian regime. The question then becomes: Why should the forces behind authoritarian rule enter such negotiations?

There can be several reasons. Democratic openings are often preceded by a split in the coalition of forces behind authoritarian rule, a split between hard-liners and soft-liners.[17] The latter may seek more democratic forms of rule—perhaps in order to get the upper hand in a conflict with hard-liners—in the face of internal and external pressures and perhaps also due to normative commitments to democracy.

More pragmatic reasons for such a move have to do with problems for which democracy can provide a solution. For example, democracy can help restore the legitimacy of the existing social order, and it can provide an open and regularized system of decision-making that can result in a better environment for conducting business. According to one scholar, "Another benefit not to be minimized is the international recognition that accompanies democratization. This can yield dividends in the form of inflows of foreign aid and loans."[18]

The point is that the elites' support of democracy is often based on self-interest; therefore, it is both fragile and conditional.[19] During the negotiations accompanying transitions toward democracy, the elites will try to stack the cards in order to make sure that the democratic institutions that are set up do not threaten their basic interests. This can be done in several ways. Adam Przeworski gave as an example the Brazilian elections held in 1982, where "the authoritarian government used every possible legal instrument to secure *a priori* advantage for the pro-government party and to secure to itself the eventual majority in the presidential electoral college."[20] These were some of the measures taken in Brazil: First, the authoritarian rulers allowed the formation of additional parties, with the aim of splitting the opposition; second, they created obstacles that made it difficult for those parties that were popular before the authoritarian rulers took over in 1964 to register; third, they made it more difficult for illiterates to cast their ballots, as they were expected to vote against the government.

Przeworski drew the somber conclusion that democratization is possible only "if there exist institutions that provide a reasonable expectation that interests of major political forces would not be affected highly adversely under democratic competition, given the resources these forces can muster."[21] In other words, elite groups will support democracy only insofar as they feel certain that their interests will be looked after under more democratic conditions. Thus, the democratic institutions that are set up as a result of negotiations with elite groups may be restricted in various ways, as, for example, is the case in Brazil. Moreover, the elite groups may require that the policies of the new, democratically based governments contain inbuilt social and economic conservatism. In summary, when transitions toward democracy are the result of negotiations with the forces behind the previous, authoritarian regime, it is likely that the new democracy will be restricted in various respects, as will be its room for maneuvering in terms of social and economic reform measures.

I shall argue later that the majority of transitions toward democracy in recent years have indeed been of this negotiated variety. Although it is clearly necessary to examine specific cases in order to study the variations in the actual compromises behind the transitions, one cannot help being somewhat pessimistic regarding the further development of democracy as well as regarding the prospects for substantial reform that would benefit the less privileged.

WHY THE RECENT SURGE TOWARD DEMOCRACY?

The previous sections have discussed the general conditions for democracy and the need to study the interplay between those conditions and the choices made by political actors. In this section, these elements are put to use in an attempt to answer the question: Why has there been a recent surge toward democracy in so many countries?

It is useful to present some information about the spread of democracy. More than thirty countries made transitions toward democracy between 1974 and 1997. The result has been a near doubling of the number of democratic regimes. The transitions began in southern Europe (Greece, Spain, and Portugal). The next wave was in Latin America (Argentina, Uruguay, Peru, Ecuador, Bolivia, Brazil, and Paraguay) and in Central America (Honduras, El Salvador, Nicaragua, Guatemala, and Mexico). Then came the transitions in Eastern Europe (Poland, Czechoslovakia, Hungary, Romania, Bulgaria, and the former German Democratic Republic). The most recent wave has been in Africa and in the former Soviet Union. Finally, transitions toward democracy have taken place in Asia over the entire period since the early 1970s (in Papua New Guinea, Thailand, Pakistan, Bangladesh, the Philippines, South Korea, Taiwan, Mongolia, and Nepal).

The changes are impressive, and they do indeed give evidence of democratic progress in a large number of countries in a relatively short span of time. But some caveats should be taken into account. First, in some countries—for example, Nigeria, Bolivia, and Cambodia—there have already been setbacks toward authoritarian rule, and since 1992 the number of countries classified as "free" by Freedom House has not risen.[22] Second, a number of the countries mentioned are not yet full democracies; they are in the early phases of a transition toward democracy, as I shall argue in further detail later. Finally, it is useful to put the democratic progress of 1974–1992 in a larger historical context. Much depends on the way in which the time periods are defined. The progress since 1974 must be seen against the background of a large number of democratic breakdowns in earlier periods, especially between the mid-1960s and the early 1970s.

In 1984, Samuel Huntington wrote that "it would be difficult to argue that the world was more or less democratic in 1984 than it had been in 1954."[23] Seen from this perspective, the democratic progress between 1974 and 1984 merely regained the distance lost by the setbacks of earlier periods. Most of the "new" democracies in Latin America, Eastern Europe, and Asia that have appeared since 1984 are thus in the category of redemocratizations, that is, returns to more democratic conditions after periods of nondemocratic rule.

Even if this is the case, the moves toward democracy in recent years are significant and must be explained. No single factor can account for these events. There are complex patterns of internal and external elements, of various conditions that interplay with different groups of actors. Moreover, the movements toward democracy in different parts of the world during the last fifteen years must be explained in different ways. Ideally, the movements should be untangled country by country, but space does not allow this. Therefore, we will look at events in major regions as well as events in some specific countries. Finally, although the question "Why has there been a recent surge toward democracy?" really covers two analytically separate issues—the breakdown of authoritarian systems and the move toward democracy instead of toward another authoritarian system—a sharp distinction between these two elements will not be made in the discussion that follows. However, I shall have more to say about the reasons behind moves toward democracy later in this chapter.

The first cluster of transitions took place in the mid-1970s in southern Europe, specifically in Greece, Portugal, and Spain. In all three cases, splits within the authoritarian regimes led to their downfall. At the same time, these countries experienced distinct phases of authoritarian breakdown followed by the erection of democracy.

In Spain, Francisco Franco had made arrangements for the continuation of authoritarian rule well before his death. Admiral Carrero Blanco was to take responsibility for the government and Juan Carlos, a monarch educated under Franco's supervision, was to become head of state. But the scheme was interrupted by the assassination of Carrero Blanco; with him out of the picture, Juan Carlos was left with a high degree of freedom to maneuver when he took over as head of state after Franco died in 1975. Carlos chose to support a process of democratization. In retrospect, it is easy to see internal and external elements conducive to change in democratic direction. Internally, a process of rapid economic growth had strengthened new social groups of workers, members of the middle classes, and students with a quest for political change. It was also becoming clear that membership in the European Union, which Spain badly wanted (as did Greece and Portugal), would require political changes. But in 1975, political democracy was only one of the options open to the main actors, and it took what one observer has called "exceptionally skilled leaders in the regime and the opposition" to negotiate the transition and further consolidate a democratic regime.[24]

In Portugal, dictator Antonio Salazar drained the country of resources by holding onto a Portuguese empire in Africa for much too long. Increasing guerrilla activity in the colonies meant that close to one-half of the national budget went to defense. Middle-ranking officers fed up with the situation staged a coup in 1974, which led to an incredibly intense period of political experimentation and debate by literally hundreds of new political groups that sprang up after the long period of authoritarian rule. The end result of political democracy appeared only in 1976.

In Greece, the transition went faster. The military colonels' junta ordered a general mobilization of troops in response to the Turkish invasion of Cyprus on July 20, 1974, but it quickly became apparent that the junta did not even enjoy the full support of its own ranks. When the Joint Chiefs of Staff decided the next day to seek a political solution to the crisis, the return of civilian rule was made possible.

The second important cluster of transitions toward democracy took place in Latin America during, roughly speaking, the first half of the 1980s. As in southern Europe, the Latin American countries felt some pressure for democracy from various organizations in Western Europe and the United States. But internal dynamics had an even greater influence. One important set of reasons concerns problems brought about by the models of economic development that were pursued under authoritarian rule. In many cases, a ruling elite coalition led by the military had used authoritarian rule to promote a strategy of economic development for the benefit of a strict minority. Production was focused on durable consumer goods for the upper middle classes (cars, consumer electronics, and so forth), and no attention was paid to the basic needs of the poor majority. By the early 1980s, these models ran into serious problems. According to one observer, the Latin American countries were "unified by crisis, foreign debt, economic stagnation . . . inflation, rising unemployment and growing social inequalities."[25] The economic crisis did not have purely domestic roots, however. The second round of sharply increasing oil prices hit most Latin American countries hard. One way to cover the increases in expenditure was to borrow more money abroad. When the real interest rate on such loans increased dramatically, as occurred during the 1980s, the economic crisis was seriously aggravated.

In some countries, with Brazil as the most important example, the authoritarian regimes could draw on records of very high rates of economic growth despite the fact that the distribution of the benefits was extremely uneven. However, when the economic crisis set in, the regimes underwent a process of **delegitimation**—that is, they could no longer point to a basis for their right to govern. In other countries (for example, Argentina and Bolivia), authoritarian rulers could not even point to achievements in terms of economic growth; characterized by corruption and incompetence, their regimes were in even more vulnerable positions.

The problems led to divisions within the authoritarian regimes—that is, the split between hard-liners and soft-liners mentioned earlier. These divisions in turn weakened the authoritarian regimes' grip on society and allowed for a process of liberalization with better possibilities for public debate, oppositional activity, and criticism of the political system. As a result, demands for democracy were reinforced and the legitimacy of authoritarian rule was further decreased. At the same time, the quest for political democracy began to receive a higher priority than ever before in many social groups in Latin America. In the days of harsh authoritarianism, there was a tendency for the polarization of forces as well as of outlooks; fascism and socialism were seen by many as the only feasible alternatives for the region. There was no possibility of a middle path. But with liberalization, the notion of political democracy gained new strength; it is supported by bishops and priests, by journalists and professors, and by labor and other social movements.[26]

In several Latin American countries, the process of democratization proceeded slowly, beginning with the regimes' liberalization. In Argentina, however, economic failures inspired the authoritarian military rulers to embark on the Falkland Islands/Islas Malvinas adventure, and the regime collapsed as a result of defeat in the war. Yet neither Argentina nor the countries that experienced a more gradual transition have fully consolidated democratic rule, as will be discussed below.

If we take one step further ahead in time, we come to the next region in which dramatic changes toward democracy have taken place: Eastern Europe. The early beginnings were in Poland, where Solidarity was founded in 1980 in an attempt by the workers to improve their economic conditions. At first, the demands were for autonomous unions, not political reform. But it quickly became clear that union autonomy could not be achieved without changes in the political system. Yet even though there were splits within the ruling party, it appeared impossible to reach agreement on a model for political reform in Poland. It was not until 1989 that the **totalitarian** regimes (authoritarian regimes in which the state attempts to control every aspect of the citizens' lives) began to fall in Eastern Europe. There had been popular uprisings on several previous occasions—in East Germany in 1952, in Hungary in 1956, and in Czechoslovakia in 1968—but they did not result in political reform. What was different in 1989? One experienced observer pointed to three basic factors, which he labeled "Gorbachev," "Helsinki," and "Tocqueville."[27]

The election of Mikhail Gorbachev signaled new Soviet policies toward Eastern Europe. Before Gorbachev came to power, the Brezhnev doctrine, which supported Soviet intervention in Eastern Europe against "unacceptable" regime changes, was in effect. Under Gorbachev, it was changed to the so-called Sinatra doctrine: "You do it your way." Gorbachev's influence can be seen more directly in the following: It was a telephone call from Gorbachev in August 1989 that urged the Polish Communists to permit the formation of a government led by a member of Solidarity (Tadeusz Mazowiecki); and when he was a guest of honor in East Germany at the country's fortieth anniversary in October 1989, Gorbachev told Erich Honecker that "the problems of DDR [Deutsche Demokratische Republik] must be solved in Berlin, not in Moscow."[28]

Yet even in the absence of Soviet assistance, the ruling elites of Eastern Europe could have sent their own troops against the popular demonstrations. Why did they hesitate? The Helsinki factor points to the Western attempt to promote respect for human rights in Eastern Europe through the Helsinki accords, which in turn opened for some countries the possibility of Western economic assistance. The Helsinki factor worked together with the Tocqueville factor. The latter points to the old ruling elite's loss of belief in its own right to rule, in its own legitimacy:

> A few kids went into the streets and threw a few words. The police beat them. The kids said: You have no right to beat us! And the rulers, the high and mighty, replied, in effect: Yes, we have no right to beat you. We have no right to preserve our rule by force. The end no longer justifies the means!
> In fact, the ruling elites, and their armed servants, distinguished themselves by their comprehensive unreadiness to stand up in any way for the things in which they had so long claimed to believe, and their almost indecent haste to embrace democratic capitalism.[29]

The popular demonstrations themselves still have to be better explained, however. The mounting economic crisis in Eastern Europe meant that the centrally planned economic system was increasingly unable to deliver dynamic performance and satisfy even the most basic needs of the population. It was a similar situation that brought Gorbachev to power in the Soviet Union. The intention on the side of the rulers was to reform and dynamize the system through more intensive cooperation with the West.

But the opening of the system posed a threat to the ruling elite: Without the important condition of isolation, the integrated power structure of the totalitarian system became much more difficult to sustain. In other words, the authoritarian political system and the centrally planned economy based on state ownership are pillars in a mutually supportive system of power, production, and distribution. Tinkering with the system at one point, such as by decentralizing economic control in order to make the enterprises cooperate with foreign firms, creates repercussions in the entire system.[30] The situation puts the ruling elites in a serious dilemma: Their attempts at reforming the system create tensions that threaten their power positions. Yet radical initiatives were necessary to prevent the socioeconomic crisis from running out of control.

The elites proved incapable of devising solutions to this dilemma. Instead, they created a moral dilemma as well. The regimes' propaganda machineries were employed to convince everyone that all was going well and that great progress was being achieved, but the message had to sound increasingly hollow to an educated population well aware of the true state of affairs. Ultimately, the gulf between truth and propaganda, between what people could say and what they thought, became intolerable. The demand for truth became as important as the demand for bread, and writers and intellectuals became the driving force in the struggle against the old regimes. The demand for improved material conditions was critical, but no less critical was the demand for freedom of the mind.[31]

Let us proceed to Africa, where the most recent transitions toward democracy have taken place. When the Berlin Wall fell in 1989, thirty-eight out of forty-five states in Africa south of the Sahara were governed by civilian or military one-party systems in various shades of authoritarianism. No more than eighteen months later, more than half of them had either held competitive multiparty elections or made commitments to do so.[32]

It is clear that the rapid changes in Eastern Europe were an important catalyst in Africa. On the one hand, those changes signaled that the cold war division, which had helped uphold nondemocratic regimes in both the Western and the Eastern camps in Africa, was coming to an end. On the other hand, they provided inspiration for the popular movements that were already mobilizing in Africa.

Thus, developments in Eastern Europe stimulated upheavals that were already under way for internal reasons, including severe economic crises, stagnation and increasing foreign debt, corruption, and economic and political mismanagement. There have also been structural changes that have increased the prospects for democratic demands: A higher degree of urbanization and of education has resulted in a population that is less bound by tradition and long-standing political leaders and that has less patience for authoritarianism.[33]

With these developments, traditional ideas about specific forms of African governance have lost currency. There were two main elements in traditional thinking: decision-making by consensus and the concept of one-party democracy. Decision-making by consensus grew out of the famous notion of the palaver tree, where people met to discuss issues for as long as was necessary, that is, until a consensus was reached. In this way, a majority could not impose its will on a minority because all individuals participated in the process. Ideally, the consensus reached by everyone would ensure that all individual differences were taken into account. The one-party system is the logical organizational framework for this kind of decision-making. In addition, the one-party system should, ideally, help to avoid the wasting of energy on fruitless political competition in an environment in which there are much more urgent tasks of economic and social development. Yet the real functioning of consensus and one-party rule has been far from the ideals. Decision-making by consensus is not applicable to large and complex societies with many different interest groups; and one-party rule has, in many cases, become a thin veil over authoritarian, corrupt rule by dictators who seek to favor themselves and their own tribes or ethnic groups.[34] The African system of personal rule will be further described later in this chapter.

In many cases, such as in Côte d'Ivoire and Gabon, incumbent leaders have seen the writing on the wall and have tried to ride with the waves of democratic change instead of being swept aside by them. They have, for example, given in to opposition demands for free elections (though it is true that they have done so at a time when opposition forces are poorly organized and unready to compete with powerful leaders with economic resources and mass media control).

One additional external factor is important in this regard: the role of the donor countries and agencies that provide the economic aid that is vital for most African states. The pressure from major donors for changes in a democratic direction as a condition for further economic assistance has been increasing in recent years. It is a piece of advice that few African countries can afford to ignore. Of particular importance is the French position, at least for Francophone Africa, which is heavily dependent on aid from France. (**Francophone Africa** is the term that describes the states in Africa that had been under French colonial rule and retain special ties with France.) In June 1990, the president of France told leaders from Francophone Africa that "the sooner you organize free elections, the better it will be for the youth of your countries who need to express themselves."[35]

Finally, there has been a domino effect in Africa: Once changes begin to occur in some countries, there is an increased likelihood that other countries will move in the same direction. A similar effect can be seen in other regions, for example in Latin America, where first Peru and then Ecuador, Argentina, Bolivia, Uruguay, and Brazil moved toward democracy within a decade. In Eastern Europe, democratization caught on even faster in a whole cluster of countries. At the same time, it is clear that the domino effect is tied to changes in international conditions that affect several countries simultaneously (for example, the change of donors' attitudes toward Africa and the new Russian policies toward Eastern Europe). It must be borne in mind, however, that these external changes have a maximum effect only when they are combined with an internal setting receptive to democracy.

It is more difficult to summarize events in Asia, where the transitions have not been clustered in a specific period but have been spread over the last two decades. Furthermore, there have also been moves away from democracy in Asia, toward authoritarianism, which makes the picture even more confusing. And countries in Asia have substantially different levels of development and therefore have different economic, social, and political structures. Even so, democracy has moved forward in recent years in the poorest and least developed of countries (Nepal), in the most well-to-do states (South Korea and Taiwan), and in countries in between (Thailand and the Philippines). There is hardly a common denominator. Three rather different cases, namely the Philippines, Nepal, and Taiwan, may demonstrate the scope of the Asian transitions in terms of both socioeconomic background and actual political processes.

The Philippines had some experience with unstable democracy before Ferdinand Marcos introduced martial law in 1972 in a society on the move toward industrialization. Yet his ploy was not totally unpopular. Martial law provided a measure of order and stability; violence by various oppositional groups decreased, agrarian reform measures and a streamlining of the administrative apparatus paved the way for a period of rapid economic growth. By 1980, however, the steam had gone out of the early measures. Rising import prices, not least for oil, a shrinking market for Philippine exports, and increasing foreign debt set the stage for an economic crisis. At the same time, Marcos and his first lady, Imelda, together with a small group of cronies, became the subject of increasing criticism because of their monopolistic control of the most important industries. The IMF was not willing to help mitigate the debt problem as long as Marcos refused to de-monopolize the economy, an act that would mean turning against his own cronies. In the countryside, the activities of Communist guerrillas increased dramatically. Yet Marcos probably could have weathered the storm had it not been for the killing of opposition leader Benigno Aquino by his own security forces. The murder caused opposition forces to rally and produced a movement for reform within the army that was sponsored by Defense Minister Juan Ponce Enrile. The murder also led to strong criticism from the United States. Marcos attempted to fence off critics by offering to compete with an opposition candidate in a free election. Corazon Aquino won the contest, albeit not with a clear mandate. At this point, Marcos tried to invalidate the election but was unable to do so, lacking internal support from the military and external support from the United States.[36]

In Nepal, the basis for democratization was radically different from the situation in the Philippines. Nepal is a small, poor country whose economy is dominated by agriculture and some tourism. It is, economically and otherwise, highly dependent on its giant neighbor, India. In early 1990, the form of regime in Nepal was absolute monarchy, as it had been for more than two hundred years. But in that year the king and his government came under pressure from three sides. First, the country had been involved in a yearlong deadlock on a trade and transit treaty with India, and the lack of a solution was beginning to create shortages of essential goods in the economy. Second, international aid donors were increasing their pressure for improvements in the human rights situation in the country. Finally, the groups in opposition to the government were inspired by the events in Eastern Europe to increase their drive for political changes, and for the first time opposition forces from the Left and the Right worked together.

The king and the government stood firm at first, instructing the police to clamp down on demonstrators and banning opposition newspapers. But as the confrontation increased, the king started leaning toward a compromise, and he eventually called upon a moderate opposition leader to form a new government. In the subsequent phase, the king and the cabinet struggled for control over the process of drafting a new constitution, which was intended to lead to a constitutional monarchy. Eventually, the king assured for himself the role of political arbiter and was empowered, for example, to declare an emergency without cabinet approval.[37]

In Taiwan, democratization has been influenced by economic success rather than failure. For many years, the state has pushed and guided economic development. Contrary to the Philippine case, politics in Taiwan has been relatively untouched by corruption and malpractice. Having lost badly to the Communists in the civil war on the mainland, Nationalist leaders were determined to clean up their act and promote rapid economic development on the island. Fifty years of Japanese colonial rule over Taiwan had left a strong infrastructure, a productive agriculture, and a population with a comparatively high level of education. Furthermore, the United States was very willing to assist Taiwan economically and otherwise as a consequence of the cold war confrontation with communism. The authoritarian regime produced a startling success in terms of economic development. But politically, it was being undermined by the very same process: Rapid economic development produces stronger social forces outside the state apparatus, including private business, the industrial labor force, and the middle classes. These developments tend to put new demands on the state. One of the important demands in recent years has been for a more democratic society. Yet the first general election, in late 1990, rewarded the government's achievements—the Nationalist party won a comfortable victory at the polls, and Nationalist leader Lee Teng Hui won the first direct presidential election in 1996.

The cases described here underline the fact that there is nothing automatic about transitions away from authoritarianism. Such transitions involve a long sequence of events in which different types of actors stand in the center of the political stage, and the final outcome is not decided beforehand. When transitions are looked at in retrospect, as we have done here, explanations for why changes occurred tend to revolve around a search for the obvious: Knowing that an authoritarian regime fell, we can try to stack all the odds that seemed to work against it and in favor of democracy. It is sobering to recall that not many years ago scholars were busily occupied with similar sequences of events going in the exact opposite direction—from more or less genuine democracies toward authoritarian rule. The exercise then was similar to the present one: Knowing that democracy broke down, one could try to stack all the odds that seemed to work against it and in favor of authoritarianism.

One way to avoid this fatalistic overtone is to demonstrate the fragility of many of the democratic openings that have taken place and to stress how they might just as easily fall back toward authoritarianism as continue toward more authentic democracy. The early transitions in southern Europe appear to be the most consolidated, whereas the recent democratic openings in Africa are the most fragile, having moved only a short distance away from authoritarianism. The mere passage of time, however, is no guarantee for a continued process of democratization. Several problems facing the current democratic openings are discussed in a subsequent section of this chapter. But first it will be helpful to introduce a model that contains a precise picture of the different phases involved in the transition from authoritarian to democratic rule.

PROCESSES OF TRANSITION AND CONSOLIDATION

The transition from nondemocracy to democratic rule is a complex process involving several phases. In the typical contemporary case, the beginning of the process is marked by crisis within and the eventual breakdown of the nondemocratic regime. If the transition to democracy begins with the realization of the authoritarian rulers that they must leave office, then this phase ends with the installation, based on free elections, of a new government.

But the process does not end there. The new regime will often be a restricted democracy, more democratic than the previous one but not yet fully democratic. Several phases of "democratic deepening" may be necessary before this latter stage is reached. And then the regime still has to be consolidated, which is said to occur when democracy is seen by all major political actors as "the only game in town." There is often considerable overlap between these phases.

It is important to realize that the phases outlined here are not necessarily negotiated in a smooth, linear manner. There may be crises and setbacks. And the result of regime change need not necessarily be democracy. The typical pattern for many developing countries has indeed been one of seesawing between authoritarianism and frail democracy.

Moreover, the full process toward consolidated democracy may take a long time, often several decades. In the case of Great Britain, the full process took more than two hundred years.

A more concrete impression of the phases and problems involved in the transition toward democracy can be attained with the use of a simple model that describes some of the main elements in the transition process (see Fig. 2.1). It is a slightly modified version of a model created by Dankwart Rustow.[38]

The model has one background condition, national unity, which must be in place before it is possible to conceive of a transition toward democ-

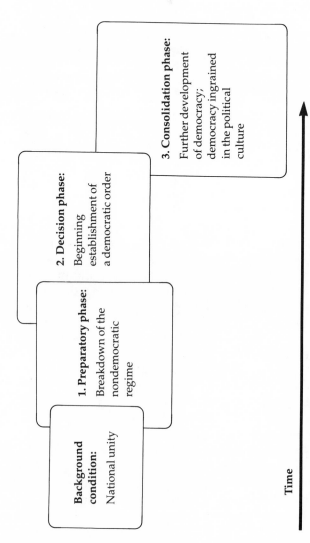

Background condition:
National unity

1. Preparatory phase:
Breakdown of the nondemocratic regime

2. Decision phase:
Beginning establishment of a democratic order

3. Consolidation phase:
Further development of democracy; democracy ingrained in the political culture

Time

FIGURE 2.1 Transitions toward democracy: A model

Source: Based on Dankwart Rustow, "Transitions to Democracy," *Comparative Politics* 2, no. 3 (1970).

racy. According to Rustow, national unity simply indicates that "the vast majority of citizens in a democracy-to-be . . . have no doubt or mental reservations as to which political community they belong to."[39] There may well be ethnic or other cleavages between groups in the population; it is only when such divisions lead to basic questioning of national unity that the problem must be resolved before a transition to democracy becomes feasible. National unity was an issue in India and Pakistan and is an issue today in Bosnia, Russia, and in several African countries. Democratization demands a settling of the national question: Who are the nations that are going to democratize?

The issue will emerge elsewhere, as well. For example, in China any process of democratization will have to settle the issue of Tibet's claim for autonomy. Empires held together by force must confront the national unity question as a precondition for a process of democratization; rulers and policies cannot change in a democratic manner if the boundaries do not endure. As one observer stated, "The people cannot decide until somebody decides who are the people."[40]

The principle also seems to apply to situations in which established democracies have to confront crises concerning national unity: If these matters are not resolved in a democratic manner (for example, through minority guarantees or local autonomy for the group in question), the result will be the breakdown of democracy combined with repression of the minority group or civil war, as in the case, for example, of Chechnya, Sudan, and Sri Lanka. Again, a return to democracy presupposes that the question of national unity is resolved.

With national unity as the single background condition, the first phase in the transition toward democracy is the *preparatory phase.* It contains first and foremost what Rustow called a prolonged and inconclusive political struggle. Some individuals, groups, and classes challenge the nondemocratic rulers. Democracy may not be their main aim; it can be a means to another end or a by-product of a struggle for other ends, such as a more equal society, a better distribution of wealth, the extension of rights and freedoms, and so forth. The composition of the groups behind the challenge to the rulers varies from country to country and also over time periods. As Rustow stated, "No two existing democracies have gone through a struggle between the very same forces over the same issues and with the same institutional outcome."[41]

The phases often overlap. In India, for example, the preparatory phase of the struggle for democracy began long before national unity and independence had been achieved. The same coalition of forces in the National Congress movement that struggled for national independence struggled for a democratic political system.

Other scholars have analyzed the preparatory phase. Alfred Stepan outlined ten different paths from nondemocratic toward democratic rule.[42] They are differentiated according to the nature of the previous authoritarian regime, the constellation of political and social forces in the various societies, and the different international contexts in which the transitions take place. The contemporary transitions toward democracy include cases of democratization initiated from within the authoritarian regimes (for example, in Latin America) as well as cases mainly triggered by external forces (for example, in Eastern Europe).

In Chapter 1, two basic dimensions of the process of democratization were identified, namely liberalization (or competition) and inclusiveness (or participation). According to the comparative study of transitions in Latin America and southern Europe by O'Donnell and Schmitter, the typical beginning of the transition to democracy is a period of liberalization. In this period, the incumbent authoritarian rulers extend a measure of civil and political rights to individuals and groups. Space for oppositional political activity (for public competition) is thereby created, albeit within a framework still controlled by the authoritarian regime. This phase began in Brazil, for example, with the suspension of press censorship in 1974. It was overlapped by a later phase of increased participation, which culminated in the election of a civilian president in 1985.[43]

A similar phase of liberalization occurred in several of the East European countries. It began with single-party pluralism, where the population was allowed to choose among different candidates of the same (Communist) party. But this development was not enough to convey legitimacy on the old rulers. In a following phase, increased opposition led to the introduction of different versions of multiparty systems in Poland, Hungary, and the Soviet Union by the late 1980s.[44]

Now let us return to our description of Rustow's model. The second phase is the *decision phase,* in which there is "a deliberate decision on the part of political leaders to . . . institutionalize some crucial aspect of democratic procedure."[45] Again, it is clear that there can be overlap with the previous (preparatory) phase. The decision may be split into several subphases. England provides a prime example of this type of incremental democratization: The compromise of 1688 started the process, and it was completed only in 1928 when suffrage was extended to women. Even when the time period is much shorter, as in Brazil, the decision phase may involve several steps. Indeed, I shall argue in a moment that many countries presently in transition toward democracy are stuck in the early phase of the decision step, having made some moves toward democracy but having far from completed the transition.

If the time period is very short, opposition forces have few opportunities to organize themselves into proper actors on the political arena. In

Romania, for example, where there was no preceding process of liberalization and where a quick outburst of popular uprising toppled the old regime, a provisional government was formed that was dominated by liberal Communists. The new rulers did not have plans for radical reforms; Romania has moved only slowly and hesitantly toward more democratic conditions.

Thus, the pace of transition influences the outcome. So does the institutional legacy of authoritarian rule. To what extent is it possible to build on political parties, interest associations, local governments, and social movements from the period of authoritarian rule? In some cases, such as Portugal and Chile, such institutions were destroyed to the extent that the government following the democratic transition had to start almost from scratch in building new institutions. In other cases, such as Brazil and Peru, structures from previous phases of democratic rule have survived and can be put to use in the transition.[46] In Eastern Europe the new regimes have hardly anything to build on, with the exception of the organizations created in some countries during the liberalization phase. Africa's problems in this regard stem from the fact that in nearly all countries experiences with democracy have been sporadic, and democratic organizations have not been effectively institutionalized.

Probably the most important factor influencing the outcome of the decision phase is the makeup of the leading coalition behind the transition. The crucial distinction is between transitions dominated by the elites who were also behind the old, authoritarian regimes, and transitions in which mass actors have gained the upper hand. The former can be called "transitions from above." As Terry Lynn Karl stated, "Here traditional rulers remain in control, even if pressured from below, and successfully use strategies of either compromise or force—or some mix of the two—to retain at least part of their power."[47] Karl stressed in her analysis of Latin American cases that transitions from above are the most frequently encountered type of transition. Insofar as there have been transitions from below, they have been unable to lead to stable democracy:

> To date, however, *no* stable political democracy has resulted from regime transitions in which mass actors have gained control, even momentarily, over traditional ruling classes. Efforts at reform from below . . . have met with subversive opposition from unsuppressed traditional elites, as the cases of Argentina (1946–51), Guatemala (1946–54) and Chile (1970–73) demonstrate.[48]

Of the recent transitions in Latin America, Karl classified those in Uruguay, Brazil, Chile, and Ecuador as transitions from above. Borderline cases are Peru and Argentina. Three further cases were also transitions from above (Mexico, Guatemala, and El Salvador), but they are in an earlier phase of moving from nondemocratic rule. In Latin America, there have been no examples of transitions from below in the last two decades that have resulted in democracy.

In a recent contribution, Karl and Schmitter argued that several of the transitions in southern and Eastern Europe can also be seen as transitions from above, although they stressed that classification is often difficult because of the complex historical patterns in single cases.[49] Examples of transitions from above in Europe include Spain, Turkey, Hungary, Bulgaria, and the Soviet Union. In the latter case, the classification is due to the controlled process of perestroika led by Mikhail Gorbachev; after the unsuccessful August 1991 coup by the old Communist elites, their influence on the transition was substantially reduced.

A transition from above may lead to a restricted democracy that is less capable than a nonrestricted democracy of making reform policies that go against vested elite interests. I shall return to this issue in a moment. The final phase of the transition to democracy must be briefly introduced first. It is the *consolidation phase*. What is consolidation? There is no agreement about the proper definition. The most demanding version states that consolidation is not reached until all the democratic institutions have been formed and the new democracy has proved itself capable of transferring power to an opposition party; it has, so to speak, proved capable of confronting the most difficult challenges. But this kind of understanding may lead to the assertion that almost no democratic regime can ever be seen as fully consolidated. Therefore, I follow the more modest definition suggested by Juan Linz, who states that a **consolidated democracy**

> is one in which none of the major political actors, parties, or organized interests, forces, or institutions consider that there is any alternative to democratic processes to gain power, and that no political institution or group has a claim to veto the action of democratically elected decision makers. This does not mean that there are no minorities ready to challenge and question the legitimacy of the democratic process by nondemocratic means. It means, however, that the major actors do not turn to them and they remain politically isolated. To put it simply, democracy must be seen as the "only game in town."[50]

Seen as a process, consolidation clearly overlaps with the decision phase. The gradual progression of decisions leading from more restricted democracy toward more real democracy can be seen as elements leading toward increased consolidation. The democratic deepening process in the decision phase is an early phase of consolidation. As long as there are major powerful groups and institutions, such as the armed forces in Latin America or the former elites (the *nomenklatura*) in Eastern Europe, that may try to circumvent or veto democratically made decisions, democracy is not fully consolidated.[51]

It can be argued that consolidation is not a purely political process but is one that also demands social and economic change. Without changes made to correct the vast inequalities in many societies, there may be decreased political support for democratically elected leaders and a "spiral of delegitimation" of the democratic regime.[52]

The final phase of consolidation is the process whereby democratic institutions and practices become ingrained in the political culture. Not only political leaders but the vast majority of political actors and of the population come to see democratic practices as part of the right and natural order of things.[53] With a few possible exceptions, this stage has not been reached in any of the transitions that have taken place in the last two decades.

*   *   *

From the background condition of national unity, the process of transition from nondemocratic rule to democracy has been described as occurring in three phases, which will most often overlap in the real world. They are the preparatory phase, characterized by a political struggle leading to the breakdown of the nondemocratic regime; the decision phase, where clear-cut elements of a democratic order are established; and the consolidation phase, where the new democracy is further developed and, eventually, democratic practices become an established part of the political culture.

It is important to stress once again that there is nothing inevitable about these phases. There is no historical law that defines this transition process as the natural order of things. As already mentioned, the natural order in many developing countries seems to be an uneasy seesaw between authoritarianism and frail democracy. Consequently, it cannot be expected that all the countries of the world will sooner or later pass through all of these stages and end up as consolidated democracies. After all, only a minority of the countries in the world can be considered democratic today. Moreover, I shall argue later that most of the newcomers in this fortunate category are plagued by serious problems.

FOUR PROPOSITIONS ABOUT
THE CURRENT TRANSITIONS TOWARD DEMOCRACY

Each transition toward democracy has its own unique characteristics. In order to know the specific conditions of each case (its distinctive constellation of forces and institutional setup) and in order to determine in what way and how far the transition toward democracy has advanced, analyses of individual countries are necessary. But a large number of case studies cannot be undertaken here. Instead, I have chosen to advance four propositions about characteristic features of the transitions in the recent surge toward democracy. Each proposition contains what I believe is an important characteristic of the large majority of these transitions. Within the context of each proposition, I will refer to concrete examples; but it is important to stress that the features described are relevant for most of the transitions currently taking place. There are only a few exceptions, which will be pointed out in due course.

My suggestion is that the large majority of the current transitions can be described as being restricted, frail and unconsolidated, and plagued by acute social and economic problems. In terms of the model outlined earlier in this chapter, these transitions are thus still in the early phases of change; the countries are seeing the breakdown of their nondemocratic regimes and the early establishment of a democratic order. In some cases (for example, Bosnia and Russia) the question of national unity is not even finally decided.

Against this rather pessimistic analysis only one encouraging element is put forward, namely that the process of popular mobilization and organization in the struggle for democracy has reached levels not seen before. This high level of mobilization and organization will make it more difficult for the new regimes to revert to more authoritarian forms of rule.

Restricted Democracies

Restricted democracies are political systems with some democratic elements but also with limits on competition, participation, and liberties. Frequently, they are characterized by the presence of elite groups whose members reserve the right to interfere in the democratic process in order to protect their interests. In the case of democratic transitions from above, such interference can be part of the actual basis of the whole movement toward democracy. In others words, the elite groups (the military, traditional economic elites, and leading politicians) may make the transition toward democracy dependent on the acceptance of a set of agreements, or **political pacts,** that define vital areas of interest for the elites. An example from Brazil may illustrate this point.[54]

An authoritarian regime led by the military came to power in Brazil in 1964. Some ten years later, a process of liberalization began, and it culminated in the formation of the New Republic with the election of a civilian president in 1985. The return of the civilian regime was orchestrated by the military in alliance with other elite groups. A series of political pacts engineered the return to civilian rule. In several important respects, these pacts serve to restrict democracy. First, the military had retained its influence in the New Republic, not only over its own affairs but also over domestic affairs. The constitutional clauses that have served as the basis for military intervention in domestic affairs remain in place. Even more important, six out of twenty-two cabinet members are uniformed officers.[55]

In addition, the New Republic has reinforced the Brazilian tradition of clientelism. Frances Hagopian stated that "guaranteed access to state resources was the price traditional elites extracted for supporting democratization."[56] The democratic opposition to authoritarian rule led by Tancredo Neves secured access to power only by promising state spoils to the traditional elites who had supported authoritarian rule. The elites were given political posts, the right to appoint federal and local state jobs, money for specific projects, and so forth. According to Hagopian, federal and state cabinets are directly based on clientelism. Therefore, these organs do not have the implementation of conceived policies as their main aim. They are geared more toward "diverting their resources to the areas of greatest political return for the ministers and secretaries that head them."[57] Political parties are also affected. They orient their activities toward this system of sharing the spoils and thereby distort the nature of political representation.

In the Brazilian case, the military is the leading force in the pact-making process. But the military is not always the dominant elite force. The negotiations between elite factions that paved the way for democracy in Uruguay in 1984 illustrate more of a compromise between dominant groups. With less influence of the military, the new democracy may have more room to maneuver; the military is less able to fully preserve its privileges and to prevent civilian control.[58]

A case that falls somewhere between Brazil and Uruguay with regard to the influence of elites on the political system is the recent transition toward democracy in Chile. The early process of liberalization was firmly controlled by the authoritarian regime under Pinochet. But the dictator lost the important plebiscite in 1988, which was supposed to secure him a new term in office. His loss paved the way for increased influence of the opposition on the transition. However, Pinochet has been able to restrict the new democracy in vital areas and preserve a high degree of influence for nondemocratic organs, among them the National Security Council and the armed forces.[59]

Overall, these variations in the influence of elite factions are a matter of degree. In all of the cases the new democracy is restricted by elite agreements about basic rules of the game. If this situation has a positive side, seen from a democratic viewpoint, it is that such agreements may be conducive to an orderly and continuous transition toward democracy.[60] The negative side, of course, is that the pacts severely restrict the democracy that comes out of the transition process. Moreover, they create a framework in which political actors may be unable to push socioeconomic reforms that would benefit the poor. This point is stressed in Terry Lynn Karl's analysis of Latin America:

> Even as these democracies guarantee a greater respect for law and human dignity when compared to their authoritarian predecessors, they may be unable to carry out substantive reforms that address the lot of their poorest citizens. If this scenario should occur . . . the democratic transitions of the 1980s that survive could prove to be the "frozen" democracies of the 1990s.[61]

Karl's remarks are less concerned with restrictions on the political system that come out of pact-making processes than with the dangers of the lack of economic change that may result from the restricted democracies. I shall return to the issue of economic consequences of democracy in the next chapter. Here it is important to stress that the lack of economic change may have serious political repercussions; namely, it may be the catalyst for a spiral of delegitimation. Ironically, then, the pact-making between elites that makes the orderly and continuous transition possible also sets the stage for a later phase of potential instability and deadlock.

Even in the absence of explicit agreements between elite factions, there can be strong forces affecting the progress of the new democratic institutions. Such forces can restrict democracy through direct intervention in the democratic process, which, clearly, can create a highly unstable political climate. The most important example of such forces in the Latin American context is of course the military, but there is frequently an interplay with civilian groups appealing to the military for intervention.

The most pressing matter affecting the military in the transition from authoritarian rule is often the issue of settling responsibility for the past. Bringing military officers to justice would seem to be a crucial task for new democratic rulers. But the military in Latin America is strong enough to avoid such moves, even in the absence of pact agreements. The situation in Argentina provides an instructive example. The military suffered a dramatic loss of legitimacy and prestige after Argentina's defeat in the war with England in 1982. The new democratic government under Raúl Alfonsin moved swiftly to penalize the armed forces and purge them of undesirable elements. For the first time in Argentina since 1930, authoritarian military rulers had to answer for their actions before a court of law. However, the summoning of active officers by the courts was more than the military could accept, and rebellions broke out in 1987. Alfonsin had to retreat from all decisions regarding punishment of the military; the only officers imprisoned were those who were behind the first juntas.[62]

Argentina is not the most extreme example. In Central American countries the military has ruled out any discussion concerning accountability for the past. In these countries, and also in Peru and Colombia where domestic violence abounds, the military is the only nationwide state authority.[63] Elected civilian governments face the imminent danger of military coups, which may be provoked for a variety of reasons, including severe economic crisis, mass movements of urban and rural poor that elude control by traditional elites, disagreement among political factions, and perceived threats to the interests of the military itself.[64]

Robert Dahl noted in his 1971 study that democracy (polyarchy) is "of course impossible unless the military is sufficiently depoliticized to permit civilian rule."[65] It is clear that this condition is far from being met in many Latin American countries today. The militaries have entered pact agreements that restrict democracy or directly intervene in the democratic process in order to safeguard what they see as vital interests, not least the preservation of their own autonomy and power.

This description of restricted democracies has focused on the transitions in Latin America. The situation with regard to new democracies in others parts of the world is not identical. But in all restricted democracies, as in the Latin American cases, there are strong forces outside the full control of the new democratic institutions, forces that in various ways restrict democratic rule.

Frail, Unconsolidated Democracies

Restricted democracies are also unconsolidated democracies, according to the definition of the elements of democracy set forth in Chapter 1. Therefore, the Latin American transitions are also examples of frail and unconsolidated democracies. This section focuses on the aspect of consolidation whereby democratic institutions and practices become ingrained in the political culture. The discussion is centered around the African transitions.

Nowhere does the consolidation of democracy face larger obstacles than in sub-Saharan Africa, where the foundation on which democracy must be built, in terms of the existing institutions of state and their positions in society, is very weak. The African state has failed both economically and politically: In general, Africans are as poor today as they were thirty years ago.[66] At the same time, the large majority of African states have so far failed to institutionalize any form of effective rule, be it authoritarianism or democracy. What is the problem?[67]

One plausible answer to this question, provided by Richard Sandbrook and also by other scholars, points to the lack of legitimacy that characterized postcolonial African states.[68] At independence, there were no strong social forces in society that were capable of disciplining political leaders. And the latter had no moral basis or legitimizing ideology from which they could demand compliance of citizens and bureaucrats. Precolonial, traditional legitimacy was no longer a relevant foundation. The type of government that filled this vacuum was a form of **neo-patrimonialism.** (Neo-patrimonialism must be understood against the background of patrimonialism, which is the name used by Max Weber to describe any type of government that originated from a royal household and that has a ruler who treats matters of state as his or her personal affair. Present-day systems of this type, such as the system of personal rule in Africa, are examples of neo-patrimonialism.)

Personal rule is based on personal loyalty, especially toward the leading figure of the regime, the strongman. All the important positions in the state, whether bureaucratic, political, military, or police, are filled with the loyal followers of the strongman, his relatives, friends, kinsmen, and tribesmen. Their loyalty to the strongman is reinforced by their sharing of the spoils of office.[69]

The strongman commands a web of informal networks, or **patron-client relationships,** within which two main forms of spoils are distributed. Both emanate from the strongman and his followers' control of the state. They are access to the state's resources in the form of jobs, contracts, favorable loans, opportunities for illegal gain, and so forth, and access to resources not directly controlled by the state but subject to state regulation, such as import permits and business licenses.

The final element in personal rule, in addition to the strongman and clientelism, is an armed force personally loyal to the regime. Because of the state's lack of legitimacy and the fact that many people are excluded from the rewards resulting from clientelism, rulers must resort to coercion or the threat of it for survival. Thus, in determining the degree of democracy in African states, one should focus less on the differences between civilian and military regimes and more on the direct and indirect political influence of the armed forces.[70]

It is against this background that different varieties of frail democracy and authoritarianism have developed in most African states. The study of regime change in Africa has aptly been characterized as "the study of the collapse of the 'tutelary' democratic regimes introduced during decolonization and the emergence of various types of authoritarian regimes."[71] The grafting of more democratic procedures, such as multiparty systems and open presidential elections, is now in the cards or has already been effectuated in many African states. But it is clear that the consolidation of democracy will be possible only if more profound changes in the structure of personal rule take place.

For this reason several scholars have stressed the need for the establishment of order, stability, and civility in the African political systems.[72] Otherwise, democracy runs the risk of deteriorating to a caricature, the direct opposite of what it claims to be in theory. According to one analysis, democracy has deteriorated in this way in Nigeria, a country of 100 million people. Corruption among politicians has swelled due to the country's income from the export of oil. "In a political climate in which the democratic control of government was regarded by politicians of all parties as a license to plunder the state, the 1983 elections deteriorated into an extended round of electoral fraud and violence. . . . Instead of controlling the government, democracy has been a method of stealing from the people."[73] Recent developments tell a similar story. The Nigerian military annulled the 1993 elections and took over once again. The military remains in power, by feeding on revenues from the country's oil and gas reserves and through violent repression and rampant corruption.

It thus remains a question of whether the democratic openings that have swept across Africa can activate the profound changes that are needed in order to consolidate democracy. What must be stressed here is the frail, unconsolidated nature of the African democratic openings. It is clear that the system of personal rule presents a very difficult background for the consolidation of democracy. One scholar, who used the term sultanistic regimes for these systems, stressed that the downfall or weakening of the leading strongman leaves "a vacuum in society that makes the establishment and consolidation of democratic politics extremely difficult."[74]

It is not hard to find evidence in support of this view from the current African scene. With the introduction of multiparty systems, swarms of political parties have been formed. They are most often separated along ethnic lines and led by individuals with no clear ideological visions but with ambitions of becoming strongmen in their own right, controlling their own political networks. Thus, 1,800 candidates of twenty-six political parties ran for election in Benin, a country of four million inhabitants. Fourteen candidates were on the ballot for the presidential election. Ninety-six parties have requested registration in Zaire. There is a real danger, then, that the democratic openings will result primarily in tugs-of-war along ethnic lines in the competition for the vacant seats of the strongmen.

That possibility holds, of course, only if the strongmen's seats are really vacant. In several cases, incumbent leaders have preempted the new winds of democracy and have succeeded in staying in power by engineering transitions from above. A recent situation in Côte d'Ivoire provides an example. Felix Houphouet-Boigny, who has been president for several decades, took the opposition by surprise in 1990 by quickly giving in to its demands for open presidential and legislative elections. In a country in which there had not been opposition activity for thirty years, twenty-six political groups were summoned by the president and told about the forthcoming elections. Opposition requests for a delay in order to gain time for getting organized were rejected—the argument was that the demand for instant elections came from the opposition itself. As a result, the election could be controlled by the president's own party, which also has a large measure of control over the media. Both the president and his party scored comfortable victories at the elections. Against this background, one may speculate whether the current pressure from Western donors for multiparty systems and political democracy in Africa can have counterproductive effects. The Western countries themselves are examples of the fact that democracy cannot be installed overnight; it is a long-term process of gradual change. When quick fixes of imposing multiparty systems, for example, are substituted for the long haul of patiently paving the way for a democratic polity, the result may be that a thin layer of democratic coating is superimposed upon a system of personal rule without changes in the basic features of the old structure.[75]

Robert A. Dahl listed five conditions that he feels are most favorable for the development of stable polyarchy—that is, stable democratic rule. They are:

- leaders do not employ the major instruments for violent coercion, notably the police and the military, to gain and maintain their power;
- a modern, dynamic, organizationally pluralist society exists;
- the conflictive potentialities of subcultural pluralism are maintained at tolerable levels;
- among the people of a country, particularly its active political stratum, a political culture and a system of beliefs exists that is favorable to the idea of democracy and the institutions of polyarchy;
- the effects of foreign influence or control are either negligible or positively favorable.[76]

With the last point being a possible exception, none of these conditions are met in the African countries today. Neither are they altogether present in the large majority of countries in Asia and Latin America or even in Eastern Europe. Against this background, there is not much hope that the recent democratic openings will progress into consolidated democracies. But it is important to note that these conditions, although the most favorable ones for the development of a consolidated democracy, are not prerequisites for its development. A relatively stable democracy is not impossible in the absence of some, or even most, of these conditions; in Africa this fact is demonstrated by the case of Botswana, which has had a democratic political system for more than two decades.[77] At the same time, the popular mobilization and organization that can be seen in the current democratic openings appear to present some hope for the future. I shall return to this idea in a moment. One final problematic characteristic of the new democracies must be introduced first.

Democracies Plagued by Acute Social and Economic Problems

The vast majority of the current transitions toward democracy face severe economic and social problems. These problems must be expected, considering the fact that economic crisis is most often an important factor behind the ousting of the earlier, authoritarian rulers. The authoritarian governments leave office, but they also leave an inheritance of acute economic problems for the new democratic administrations to tackle.

The 1980s has been called the lost decade in Latin America because in many countries the average real income per capita returned to the level of the late 1970s. The decisive factor in the Latin American crisis is the spiraling foreign debt. By 1987, the debt burden had reached 46 percent of the region's gross national product (GNP) and more than four times the value of its exports. In addition to the debt, the countries have been faced with the problems of trying to curb inflation while trying to avoid stagnation and rising unemployment.

The economic and social crisis is even more severe in Africa. In many countries the problem is one of mere survival in the face of famine and drought. They have increasingly relied on aid from donors, both international organizations and single countries in the North. In this context it is important to note that no additional aid seems to be forthcoming as a result of the democratic openings. Current public opinion in the North seems to be that starvation and death are more acceptable in Africa than elsewhere or are unavoidable there. In other words, the conditions that are being imposed concerning democratization do not promise more aid if they are met; they promise less aid if they are not met.

Although social and economic crisis is a factor in most of the current transitions toward democracy, the focus in this section is on Eastern Europe. The political transitions there take on a special significance because they must transpire in the context of a profound change in the economic structure. This change, in turn, will deeply affect the entire social profile of society and thus the whole basis for democratic regimes. Moreover, there is no available blueprint or model for the economic transition from a centrally planned economy to some form of capitalism.

The planned economies have been locked in an evil circle of stagnation, lack of innovation, and low productivity. The days are long gone when people believed in the official *Polish Encyclopedia* definition of economic crisis, according to which "crisis is a phenomenon solely connected with the capitalist economies and does not occur in other socioeconomic systems."[78] Earlier attempts at injecting change into the planned economies left the groundwork of the system basically unchanged. The current metamorphosis, in contrast, aims at transforming the basic pillars of the system. Three fundamental economic changes must take place so that the economies are transformed (1) from being closed to being integrated in the world market; (2) from being centrally planned to being market guided; and (3) from being collectively and state owned to being based on private ownership.

With regard to the first necessary transformation, gradual openings toward the world market began in some countries, such as Hungary, long before the political events of 1989. What is in the cards now is a much faster and more comprehensive process of world market integration than seen earlier. Judged on the basis of previous experiences, the transition is going to be difficult. Demand for all kinds of imports in Eastern Europe far exceeds the countries' capacity for exporting. Several export articles, moreover, such as textiles and foodstuffs, must compete with traditional industries of southern European members of the European Union, which makes market access difficult. The result of high import needs combined with low export capacity is rapidly increasing foreign debt, as has already been demonstrated in Poland and Hungary. In those countries, debt amounts in relation to exports had already reached Latin American levels by the mid-1980s. Thus, even though this period is one of rapidly rising expectations in the Eastern European populations, those countries must curb imports because they are unable to pay for them. In this context, one of the serious criticisms against the IMF stabilization programs (for example, in Poland) is that they are more directed toward maintaining a country's external economic balance than toward securing a smooth overall transformation of the economy.

The second basic transformation is from centrally planned control to economies based on the market forces. The problem here is that the mere retreat of central planning does not in itself leave the economy with a smoothly functioning free market. A market economy functions only if it is backed by the necessary institutional and legal frameworks. Needed, for example, are an independent banking system that can provide credit for enterprises at levels determined strictly by commercial criteria; an unemployment support system, without which the dismissal of workers and the shutdown of unproductive enterprises on a large scale is unfeasible; and a legal back-up system that can lay the ground rules for free competition among firms. These systems cannot be created overnight; and in the transition period between one system and the other, which may take several years or even more than a decade, there is ample room for profiteering, speculation, and black market activity.

Another aspect of the transition toward a market-based economy has to do with the attitudes of the population. The introduction of the market system will be accompanied by rapidly increasing inequalities, widespread unemployment, and sharply rising prices; yet the wages of many employees will remain relatively fixed. As one scholar has put it, it is simply not possible to meet the economic challenges and simultaneously "provide the population with administrative guarantees of a life without losses and conflicts."[79] All of this goes squarely against the deeply ingrained egalitarian social values held by substantial parts of the populations.[80] Consequently, the issue arises about the extent to which the populations are ready to support such changes. In the long run, when the benefits of change will be more readily apparent, there may be no problem. But in the short and medium run, the economic changes constitute a "valley of tears" for which enthusiastic support by the large, negatively affected groups, may not be forthcoming.[81] Therefore, one cannot assume that there will be a straightforward, mutually reinforcing relationship between democratization in the political sphere and changes toward a market economy in the economic sphere in Eastern Europe; it is quite possible that large groups may use their newly gained political influence to resist rapid economic change.[82] Such resistance may in turn undermine the socioeconomic basis for a consolidated democratic order because such an order cannot be built without profound economic changes.

The final element in the economic transformation of Eastern Europe, the move from collective, state-owned enterprise to a system based on private ownership, is plagued by major practical difficulties because few, if any, private citizens are capable of or interested in buying the large industrial enterprises. Thus, there has been discussion in several countries about issuing peoples' shares or giving away the enterprises to the employees. But there is another, more precarious aspect of this transformation. When privatization of state enterprises is combined with the elimination of the central planning machinery, the very power basis of the old elite is undermined. To what extent will the old party-state apparatus resist such changes by sabotaging reform programs, and what will the consequences be for the fledgling democracies?

There are no straightforward answers. The power of the old elites in Eastern Europe, the *nomenklatura,* has been compared to the power of the military in Latin America. In these terms, the Latin American democracies worry about "the *Gorrilla* question," and the new democracies in Eastern Europe worry about "the *nomenklatura* question."[83] The countries find themselves in a precarious balance: When the old elites retain a high degree of influence on the transition process, the result is the restricted democracies identified in the Latin American context. If they are cut off from influence, they may utilize whatever remains of their power positions to destabilize the new, fragile democracies.

In this sense, the current situation in Eastern Europe is at an impasse: A potential, virtuous circle in which economic reform is reinforced by a process of democratic consolidation stands against a potential, vicious circle of democratic decay reinforced by economic crisis. The outcome is far from certain; most probably it will vary across countries. It is clear, however, that a smooth passage for the Eastern European countries toward consolidated democracies and sound economies capable of meeting the demands for higher standards of living cannot be taken for granted. For some countries in Eastern Europe, the future may just as easily be a Latin American version of reality. One scholar has succinctly outlined this perspective:

> Forget for a moment the geographical location and put Poland in the place of Argentina, Hungary in the place of Uruguay. You will see states weak as organizations, political parties and other associations that are ineffectual in representing and mobilizing, economies that are monopolistic, over-protected and over-regulated, agricultures that cannot feed their own people, public bureaucracies that are overgrown, welfare services that are fragmentary and rudimentary. And would you not conclude that such conditions breed governments vulnerable to pressure from large firms, populist movements of doubtful commitment to democratic institutions, armed forces that sit menacingly at the sidelines, church hierarchies torn between authoritarianism and social justice, nationalist sentiments vulnerable to xenophobia?[84]

But the countries of Eastern Europe are not doomed to failure; neither are those of Latin America, Africa, or Asia. One of the most encouraging elements in the recent democratic openings is the process of popular mobilization and organization that has taken place in the context of the fight for democracy. This theme is explored in the following section.

Popular Mobilization and Organization in the Struggle for Democracy

The three propositions presented so far paint a rather gloomy picture of the current processes of transition toward democracy. But there is also a more promising aspect, which is the focus here. It concerns popular mobilization and organization. The discussion earlier in this chapter of transitions from above may have conveyed the impression that regime change is often imposed by competing elites on a docile population that is inarticulate in political matters. Such a picture is false. Even in the cases where elites dominate the process of transition, there is a large measure of popular activity. So-called ordinary men and women, workers, students, peasants, and office clerks are taking risks in distributing propaganda against authoritarian regimes, are organizing illegal groups, and in some cases are even directly assaulting the seats of power.[85]

In some cases the different movements come together in a popular upsurge, where diverse groups from all corners of society join together to form a greater whole, identifying itself as "the people" and demanding democracy and the removal of the old rulers.[86] But the point to be stressed here is that the process of popular mobilization and organization is more than this brief, intense outburst that dies away quickly. It begins during authoritarian rule and continues in a new setting after the first elections have taken place. In that sense, the popular mobilization behind a transition toward democracy includes two different elements: the new social movements that emerged as various types of self-help organizations during authoritarian rule and the overall resurrection of civil society that takes place during the transition itself.

The term new social movements encompasses a wide range of rural and urban associations. In the Latin American context, self-help projects concerning housing, community health care, popular education, consumer and producer cooperatives, and the defense of rural land rights have emerged, as have activities of "protest and conflict, lobbying and pressuring government agencies and politicians."[87] In Africa, a similar array of groups, together with ethnic and kinship associations and regional or hometown groupings, has emerged.[88] The new social movements have often appeared because of the difficulties created by authoritarian rule; the self-help organizations are a strategy of survival. Some of the organizations in Africa are working outside the formal economy in an attempt to cater to basic needs locally or in cooperation with nearby communities.[89]

During the transition phase these new social movements are joined by human rights groups, amnesty committees, and other civil associations; in some countries in Latin America, the justice and peace commissions of the Catholic church have played an important role. Their critique of the authoritarian regimes' abuses combined with their demands for democracy help to secure basic political, legal, and social rights. Finally, during the transition process the organizations of civil society that were suppressed during authoritarian rule often reappear on the political stage, including trade union associations, professional groups (lawyers, engineers, social workers, journalists, and so forth), and university associations.

The emergence of a stronger civil society in the context of the struggle for democracy has a wider perspective. These diverse associations constitute the plural society that is an important precondition for a thriving democracy because they create power centers outside the state. Moreover, their internal organizations create forums for the education of citizens in democratic decision-making. In this sense, the associations can act as "seedbeds of democracy."[90]

Thus, the transition toward democracy creates a more open environment in which the associations of civil society have much better possibilities for functioning. But the changes in society cause questions to be raised about the relationship between the movements and the emerging

political parties. In many cases, the new social movements were organized in direct opposition to the state apparatus and orthodox party politics. Yet the best way to support the nascent democracy seems to be by becoming active in the political parties.

In Brazil, for example, this issue has divided many of the grassroots
movements. But there is evidence that a large number of activists have
gone into party politics since the early 1980s. Some observers have argued that this trend signifies a substantial strengthening of the Brazilian
party system because it helps move the parties away from their earlier
role as clientelistic machines centered on the advancement of individual
leaders. In other words, an institutionalization of the party system is taking place, which provides a stronger basis for democracy in Brazil: "The
influx of movement activists into the party system . . . brought an ideological coherence and structuring to the system that is entirely novel in
Brazilian politics."[91]

The pattern of popular mobilization and organization in the Eastern
European transitions has been radically different from that in Latin America. In Eastern Europe the associations of a civil society were nearly
nonexistent before the transitions began (the church is the only major exception); all aspects of people's lives, from cradle to grave, took place in
the context of organizations that were linked with the party-state apparatus. Therefore, the democratic demands did not come from a medley of
different associations; such associations simply did not exist. The decisive
dividing line was between "them," the party-state elite, and "us," the
people. The democratic demands came from the people, and the organizational structures corresponded to this all-encompassing showdown;
the popular organizations simply included all of the people—Civic Forum in Czechoslovakia, Neues Forum in East Germany, Solidarity in
Poland. But the demands of the people, in turn, were for the very right to
organize in a civil society, to form associations outside the control and interference of the party-state. This process has now begun, with the socioeconomic changes previously discussed, and it is clearly a long-term undertaking; one scholar has ventured that it is going to take at least one
generation.[92]

The flurry of popular activity briefly described here does not apply in
equal measure to all the current transitions toward democracy. In many
cases in Africa and elsewhere, the democratic openings have been a dis-
tinctly urban affair, and popular activity has been sporadic. Yet the overall picture is quite clear: The transitions toward democracy are accompanied by decisive upsurges in popular mobilization and organization. A
strengthening of civil society is taking place, which improves the conditions for democracy and simultaneously makes the reversal to authoritarian rule more difficult.

At the same time, however, the transition toward democracy creates a new political environment with new challenges to the popular movements. The rallying point of a common enemy—the authoritarian government—is no longer there. The challenge has shifted from cooperating in a common goal of removing old rulers to working toward institutionalizing a democratic competition between the interests and visions of various groups in the population. The demands put on the skills and commitments of leading actors to meet this challenge are different from those required during the transition itself. The actors must, according to one observer of Latin America, "demonstrate the ability to differentiate political forces rather than to draw them all into a grand coalition, the capacity to define and channel competing political projects rather than seek to keep potentially divisive reforms off the agenda, and the willingness to tackle incremental reforms . . . rather than defer them to some later date."[93] In other words, the popular mobilization and organization in itself improves the prospects for democracy; but the way this popular power is utilized is a decisive element in the difficult process that will determine whether democracy will be consolidated.

APPROACHING THE MILLENNIUM—
PROSPECTS FOR DEMOCRACY

This chapter has discussed many transitions toward democracy. The transitions began in southern Europe in the 1970s and came to include Latin America in the early 1980s and then Eastern Europe, Africa, and parts of Asia in the late 1980s and early 1990s. The wave of democratization began in Europe (Spain, Greece, and Portugal) and ended in Europe, in the sense that many of the countries undergoing the most recent transitions are also European (e.g., Russia and some of the former Soviet republics as well as Bosnia and Serbia of former Yugoslavia).

What is the current status of these transitions to democracy as we approach the new millennium? The four propositions previously set forth amount to a somewhat pessimistic evaluation of the democratic prospects for these countries. Is such pessimism warranted, given the developments in the 1990s?

The most spectacular setbacks for early and frail democratic openings have been in sub-Saharan Africa, where ethnic violence in some cases has led to the breakdown, not merely of the sprinkles of democracy but of state authority altogether, as in Rwanda, Somalia, and Sudan. I will have more to say about these conflicts in Chapter 4. Yet even in poor and crisis-ridden Africa, signs of progress exist. Democracy is becoming more consolidated in South Africa, and democratic institutions are being strengthened in Botswana, Namibia, Benin, and Mali. These are positive signs more than certain indicators of success, however. To talk about any firm and irreversible democratic consolidation is still premature.

With the exception of some African countries, there has been no comprehensive decay of democracy. There may not have been any startling successes either—in the form of smooth and rapid democratic consolidation—yet on the surface of things, it seems that democratization is hanging on, even slowly progressing in some countries. Is that the best we can hope for, and should we then not be more optimistic? The answer to that question is unfortunately no. Although extensive democratic decay has not occurred, the majority of the current democratizations are of the restricted, elite-dominated variety described previously and known as **frozen democracies.**

Take Latin America, for example, where one scholar has recently emphasized how the democratic transitions are developing into a hybrid form of democratic-authoritarian system that he calls "market authoritarianism." In this system, "the trappings of formal democracy are retained and the tenets of market economics . . . are generally followed. But in response to mounting social unrest rule is more by decree than consent, media critical of government is bullied and power is maintained through corruption, intimidation and, ultimately, by force."[94] Economic reforms have worked in Latin America, at least in bringing some measure of stability and lowering inflation; in that sense, the fundamental economic outlook is hopeful. But, as one observer has stressed, "the poor cannot eat 'fundamentals.' "[95] Income gaps are widening, the absolute number of people living in poverty is increasing, real wages have fallen, and unemployment is higher than in 1990. An authoritarian takeover by the military is not likely, but military and police forces continue to hold privileged positions in the region; spending on security exceeds total welfare spending, while political control of the military remains insufficient. Most courts are corrupt and inefficient, and in many Latin American countries groups of police are a source of threat rather than a source of protection for the population.

Elite domination and increasing popular despair also characterize Eastern Europe and particularly Russia. The former Communist elites, the *nomenklatura,* have not blocked economic and political reforms. Instead, they have chosen another strategy: to exploit old positions and networks in transforming themselves into the new, market-oriented economic and political elite. Rather than preventing reforms, the old elites are swimming with the tide and emerging as owners of newly privatized companies, often acquired cheaply with the help of old friends. The old elite also continues to dominate state bureaucracies and in recent years has regained political power with the help of newly formed, non-Communist parties.

Why do people vote for former Communists? Because they promise to make people rich; "they represent success: more than any other identifiable social group in Eastern Europe, they are seen to have achieved the most in the new regime."[96] Former Communists no longer represent the past; they represent the successful capitalist future. What is the problem then? Is it not ideal that the forces of the past are becoming the architects of the future? The problem is that only a few of the new entrepreneurs hold traditional capitalist virtues, such as hard work, honesty, and responsibility. It is sooner a "corrupt business class which is intimately intertwined with a corrupt political class." The end result is "some forms of robust private entrepreneurship, an enormous, untaxed, gray market, and large companies, some state-owned some private, which enjoy deeply corrupt relationships with powerful politicians. Various forms of criminal mafia will dominate some parts of the region; politicians will come to 'represent' various business interests, as they clearly do already, particularly in Russia."[97] There are some positive elements in this otherwise gloomy picture of Eastern Europe. Economic and political relations with Western Europe are developing rapidly. The attraction of closer cooperation with the European Union will help prevent any across-the-board deterioration of democratic conditions. In that sense, Eastern Europe's external environment is conducive to democracy.

That is not the situation in South and East Asia. In China, economic growth rates remain high, but corruption among political and economic elites is an increasing problem. Political repression of any dissident voices is swift and severe and has included numerous executions. Corruption is a central problem in many other Asian countries as well, including Thailand, the Philippines, and Indonesia.

India has experimented with market-oriented economic reforms in recent years, which has created some increased economic dynamism. But benefits have not reached the approximately 400 million Indians who are poor, and the resulting popular discontent is being tapped by Hindu nationalist parties. This situation has led to political fragmentation and severe communal violence. India will not disintegrate, however, as have some of the very weak African states, but Indian democracy has suffered in the process, and the political scene in several Indian states is dominated by militant groups or even by criminal gangs, as is the case in Bihar.

In sum, frozen democracy in the form of "market authoritarianism" characterizes a large number of the current democratic transitions. This is not an argument against a market economy, but it does underscore how the popular majorities are suffering from the unregulated, corrupt, and elite-dominated ways in which the market forces are being introduced. There is hope in some countries that the changes brought about by economic growth (e.g., increased wealth, better education, a larger middle class) will eventually bring better conditions for democracy. Some countries also have the institutional capacity for improving the current state of affairs (see Chapter 3). But from a democratic point of view, most of the nations in transition are not doing well as we approach the millennium.

CONCLUSION

In this chapter we have studied processes of democratization, first in a general sense and then with a focus on the current transitions toward democracy. It was stressed that it is impossible to draw up a general law to the effect that democracy will always emerge provided certain preconditions are present. It is more productive to conceive of an interplay between social, cultural, economic, and other conditions, on the one hand, and decisions taken by political actors, on the other.

No single factor can account for the contemporary surge toward democracy. Each case involves a complex pattern of internal and external elements; in each, various conditions interplay with different groups of actors. Furthermore, the movements toward democracy in different parts of the world during the last fifteen years must be explained in different ways. Within the scope of this book it is not possible to unravel the processes country by country. Therefore, we looked at events in major regions of the world and reviewed a few specific country examples in detail. One must always keep in mind the danger caused by hindsight: Explaining past events can easily become a search for the obvious because we already know what happened.

In more general terms, the process of transition to democracy can be described with a simple model. The background condition of the model is national unity, and the overlapping phases of the transitions are (1) the preparatory phase, characterized by a political struggle leading to the breakdown of the nondemocratic regime; (2) the decision phase, where clear-cut elements of a democratic order are established; and (3) the consolidation phase, where the new democracy is further developed, and, eventually, democratic practices become an established part of the political culture.

The phases do not represent a predetermined path that all countries will or must follow. There is no historical law that says that regimes must move from authoritarian to democratic; a more accurate description of the typical pattern in the developing world is an uneasy fluctuation between authoritarianism and frail democracy.

It was argued that the large majority of the current transitions are in the early phases of moving toward democracy. More specifically, they can be described as restricted democracies that are frail and unconsolidated and plagued by acute social and economic problems. The only characteristic of the transitions that paints a more optimistic picture is that the process of popular mobilization and organization in the struggles for democracy has reached higher levels than seen before, thereby making reversals to authoritarianism more difficult.

When an overall assessment is made, one must be skeptical about the prospects for many of the new democracies. The large measure of elite influence in the early stages of the move away from authoritarianism can lead to a later phase of instability and stalemate during which it can prove impossible to further develop and strengthen democracy. Furthermore, the optimal conditions for the consolidation of democracy are not present in the large majority of the new democracies. Finally, the economic and social crisis that exists in these countries makes a smooth passage toward consolidated democracy even more difficult.

It may well be that determined groups of actors will be able to consolidate democracy in some countries, despite the generally adverse conditions. The transition in Spain is an example, as is the transition in South Africa. But Spain also had the external incentive of a European Community demanding democratization as a membership condition; and South Africa's economic development is much stronger than that of other African countries, thus favoring its transition to democracy.

In the developing world, only a few countries thus present reasonably favorable conditions for democratic consolidation. The general picture is much more gloomy; in most cases, the odds seem to weigh heavily against the further development and consolidation of the frail democratic openings that have taken place in recent years. These openings inspired a wealth of analyses on transitions toward democracy. Unfortunately, there is imminent risk that the next set of analyses will deal with democratic decay rather than democratic consolidation.

THREE

□   □   □

Domestic Consequences of Democracy: Growth and Welfare?

Is democracy really worth the trouble? Does it pave the way for improvements in spheres of life other than those narrowly connected with political freedoms? For the populations of the countries currently undergoing transitions toward more democratic rule, this issue is painfully crucial. This chapter looks at consequences of democracy with regard to economic development, which we will define as growth and welfare. The relationship between democracy and human rights is also addressed. Whereas democracy was treated as a dependent variable in Chapter 2, where we were looking for conditions favorable to the rise of democracy, democracy is treated as an independent variable in this chapter, where we are looking at its effects on economic development. In this chapter, we will consider the question of whether democracy, once it is attained, will be able to fulfill expectations of improved performance in terms of economic growth and welfare. The scholars who have addressed this issue are not all optimists; some even see a trade-off between political democracy on the one hand and economic development on the other. The main standpoints in the theoretical debate are outlined, and a survey of the empirical studies addressing the question is provided.[1] It will reject the notion of a general trade-off between democracy and economic development, but I will also demonstrate why economic development and welfare improvement will not necessarily be forthcoming from the new democracies.

THE DEBATE ON DEMOCRACY AND DEVELOPMENT

Many scholars see an incompatibility between democracy and economic growth for both economic and political reasons. The economic reasons relate to the fact that growth requires an economic surplus available for in-

64

vestment. Such a surplus can be either invested or consumed. Hence, the only way to increase the investable surplus is to reduce consumption. The argument is that a democratic regime will not be able to pursue policies of curbing consumption (holding down real wages) because the consumers are also voters, and they will punish the politicians next time they get the chance at the ballot box. Therefore, in a democratic system, political leaders have to cater to the short-term demands of the population. In the words of an Indian economist: "Under a system in which lawmakers . . . seek the approval of the electorate, the politician cannot afford . . . to follow any policies which will not produce tangible benefits for the electorate by the time the next election comes around."[2]

Accordingly, there is an incompatibility in the short and medium run between economic growth (investment) and welfare (consumption): You cannot have your cake and eat it too. Those who have economic reservations about democracy focus on the tendency for democratic leaders to be persuaded by the electorate to promote too much welfare and, consequently, too little growth. Their actions jeopardize the whole basis for welfare promotion in the long run.

Those with political reservations about democracy take as their starting point the fact that economic development is best promoted when there is a high degree of political stability and order.[3] Democracy is counterproductive in this regard because it opens the already weak institutions of the developing countries to all kinds of pressures from different groups in society. Instability and disorder are the result, especially in countries in which there is a massive potential for conflict stemming from numerous religious, ethnic, regional, and class divisions. In other words, the policies for change that have the objective of long-run national development can best be promoted by governments insulated from the crisscrossing political pressures of a democratic polity. In that sense, authoritarianism is best suited for the promotion of change.[4]

Another argument that scholars have made to show that authoritarian rule is better suited than democracy to promote economic development is based on the fact that the odds are increasingly being stacked against the successful promotion of development and thus the demands for comprehensive state action in order to promote development have increased dramatically over time. There is more competition from the world market and a higher internal urgency for development than was the case when the industrialized Western countries went through the early phases of development. Indeed, the processes of development then and now are qualitatively different. And in this century there has been no case of successful economic development without comprehensive political action involving massive state intervention in the economy. Such concerted state action is difficult, if not impossible, under democratic conditions.[5]

The current tasks of nation-building are indeed formidable. "It is almost inconceivable how the process can be managed without recourse to dictatorship," exclaimed one scholar,[6] and his words succinctly summarize the position of those seeing an incompatibility between democracy and economic development. At the same time, it must be stressed that the trade-off is seen as a temporary one. Political order and governmental authority are needed in order to get through the early, difficult stages of economic development. Only at a later stage do participation and distribution become relevant. The position was summarized neatly by Gabriel Almond and G. Bingham Powell: "State building and economy building are logically prior to political participation and material distribution, since power sharing and welfare sharing are dependent on there being power and welfare to share."[7]

Critics of the viewpoint that there is a trade-off between democracy and economic growth challenge all of the arguments that have been set forth. They counter the economic argument about democracy hurting growth as follows. Although it is true that a specific amount of economic surplus can be either invested or consumed but not both, the conclusion that there is thus sharp contradiction between growth and welfare is not as straightforward as it seems. For example, public expenditure in such areas as health and education constitutes investment in human capital, which simultaneously improves welfare for large groups in the population. Indeed, many economists advocate a strategy of development that emphasizes basic human needs because in that area it is possible to have growth and welfare simultaneously.[8] If we can have simultaneous growth and welfare, the argument in favor of authoritarianism because of democracy's tendency to promote too much welfare weakens severely. Indeed, the choice may be not between growth and welfare but between two different kinds of investment policy—one that supports welfare and one that does not. And it can be argued that a democratic government is more likely to promote the former policy and an authoritarian government, the latter.[9]

Next, the critics turn the argument that democracy cannot secure order and stability on its head by pointing out that authoritarianism can mean arbitrary rule and undue interference in citizens' affairs. Only a democracy can provide the predictable environment in which economic development can prosper. Moreover, political and economic pluralism reinforce each other. Without basic civil and political liberties, citizens will not feel secure to consistently pursue economic goals.[10] In that sense, there is a mutually reinforcing relationship between democracy and economic development.

Finally, there is the argument concerning the need for comprehensive and concerted state action in order to promote economic development. Although strong state action may be needed, it cannot be taken for granted that a strong state capable of taking a leading role in economic development efforts is also necessarily a nondemocratic state. In other words, a strong state and an authoritarian state are not synonymous. A strong state has an efficient and noncorrupt bureaucracy, a political elite willing and able to give priority to economic development, and well-designed policies for pursuing development goals. A strong state in this sense is not necessarily authoritarian.[11] The argument concerning democracy's effects on economic development are summarized in Figure 3.1.

In sum, the view of the critics is not so much that democracy is invariably better suited for promoting economic development than is authoritarian rule (for there may be cases in which authoritarian rule has helped produce a faster rate of growth during certain periods). The view is that the arguments presented by those advocating a trade-off between democracy and development are simply not strong enough to support a general claim of the superiority of authoritarianism for economic development. In other words, democracy and development cannot be seen as generally incompatible even if there are some cases of fast growth under authoritarian conditions. Some countries with harsh authoritarian rule have not shown the economic development benefits identified by the trade-off advocates.

So is there a trade-off between democracy and development? A fairly large number of analyses have been conducted in an attempt to answer this question, yet the answer remains inconclusive.[12] Perhaps the most comprehensive study is a survey by Robert Marsh of the performance of ninety-eight countries between 1955 and 1970. He concluded that "political competition/democracy does have a significant effect on later rates of economic development; its influence is to *retard* the development rate, rather than to facilitate it. In short, among the poor nations, an authoritarian political system increases the rate of economic development, while a democratic political system does appear to be a luxury which hinders development."[13] A similar conclusion was reached by Yousseff Cohen following his study of economic growth in a number of Latin American countries.[14]

Dirk Berg-Schlosser, in his analysis of African regimes, stated that authoritarian systems have a "strong positive effect on the overall rate of GNP growth,"[15] but he also emphasized that democratic (polyarchic) regimes have done better than should be expected: "Thus polyarchic systems fare quite well both in terms of GNP growth and the improvement of the basic quality of life. They also have the best record concerning normative standards (protection of civil liberties and freedom from political repression)."[16] Dwight King reached a similar conclusion in his study of six Asian countries: "If performance is evaluated in terms of material equality and welfare rather than growth, and is examined diachronically over the past decade and within differentiated population groups (rural,

	Democracy impedes economic development	Democracy can promote economic development
Economic reasons	Democracy is unable to reduce consumption in favor of investment. Thus, economic growth suffers.	Democratic investment in basic human needs is good for economic growth.
Political reasons	Democracy increases the pressure on weak institutions. Concerted state action is more difficult. The state is weak.	Democracy provides a stable political environment and the basis for economic pluralism. Democracy means legitimacy: A strong state is often also a democratic state.

FIGURE 3.1 Democracy: Does it promote or impede economic development?

landless, and near landless), democratic-type regimes (Malaysia, Sri Lanka) have performed better than bureaucratic-authoritarian ones (Indonesia, Philippines, Thailand)."[17]

G. William Dick examined the growth record of seventy-two countries between 1959 and 1968. He categorized the countries according to their form of government: authoritarian, semi-competitive, or competitive. He readily admitted that the data are not unambiguous, but he maintained that the "results certainly do not support, and tend to refute, the view that authoritarian countries are universally capable of achieving faster economic growth in the early stages of development than countries having competitive political systems."[18]

Thus, as mentioned earlier, no clear answer to the trade-off question emerges from these studies, and it seems that there is little help to be had from the review of additional analyses, as a recent survey has demonstrated.[19] The question inevitably arises of whether it is really a meaningful exercise to seek a definite answer through these largely quantitative analyses of large numbers of cases covering limited periods of time. Dick's contribution provides a good example of the problems involved. First, it does not seem reasonable to base such an analysis on a period covering less than a decade. The economic performance of developing countries varies substantially over time, and nine years is not a representative period. Second, whereas a small number of cases would not be representative, a large number of cases invariably presents problems with regime classification. The best growth performers in Dick's analysis are the so-called semi-competitive countries. According to the definition he used and data from 1970, Algeria, Ethiopia, South Africa, and Nicaragua under Anastasio Somoza are classified not as authoritarian but as semi-competitive. But one can easily argue that such regimes should be considered authoritarian, and then the whole basis for Dick's conclusion would disappear.

The other contributions are plagued by similar problems. Thus, what we learn from these analyses is that there are a large number of countries that are not clearly identifiable as democratic or authoritarian and that countries move very fast between the categories, being semi-democratic yesterday, authoritarian today, and semi-democratic tomorrow. Each time they make a stop in one of the categories, they lend their economic performance data, often covering only a few years, to a different argument in these investigations.

If all the overwhelming methodological problems could be solved, would it then be possible to come up with a universally relevant answer to the trade-off question? I contend that it is impossible to arrive at a law-like statement concerning the effects of regime form on economic development. How can we say "When this is the form of regime, democratic or authoritarian, we can expect such and such in terms of economic development" when very dissimilar entities are covered by the label democratic and by the label authoritarian? I am not saying that the form of regime is irrelevant for economic development. But when theorizing on the relationship, we need to be less ambitious, in the middle range. Instead of attempting to make universal statements about the relationship between regime form and economic development, we should look for systematic relationships between development outcomes and *different types* of democratic and authoritarian systems, and we should study outcomes in comparable pairs of democratic and authoritarian cases.

Both of these pathways are tried out in the sections that follow. We will look first at a pair of comparable cases, one authoritarian and one democratic, and then at different types of authoritarian and democratic systems.[20]

INDIA VERSUS CHINA

India and China are very large, populous, and predominantly agrarian countries. They both had a rather low level of social and economic development in 1950, following India's independence in 1947 and the Chinese revolution in 1949. Today, India has a long tradition of democratic rule, whereas China has been under socialist authoritarianism since the Communist victory in 1949. It may be that India's democracy is less than perfect and that some democratic elements have been present in China (see Chapter 1), but the overall difference is clear. Thus we have a democratic and an authoritarian country that have had stable regime forms for more than three decades and that have a number of basic traits in common, including similar levels of development in 1950. They are good candidates for comparing development outcomes of democratic and authoritarian regimes.

Economic development as defined here includes two elements, growth and welfare. Let us first look at the economic growth of China and India, shown in Table 3.1. We must bear in mind that growth statistics are seldom fully reliable, and there is also a problem with comparability.[21]

Although the exact magnitudes of the growth rates are in question, we have no reason to doubt that the overall growth rate in China has been substantially higher than in India. On one important dimension the difference is not dramatic—namely, agricultural growth between 1950 and 1980. Before discussing this point further, let me make a few more general remarks on the growth figures.

The data in Table 3.1 seem to fully confirm the trade-off argument insofar as authoritarian China has achieved much higher growth rates than has democratic India. Those who believe that there is a trade-off between democracy and economic growth would probably contend that the authoritarian Chinese regime has consistently held down consumption and given first priority to investment. Morever, the regime has been able to avoid disorder and instability while consistently pursuing a strategy of rapid change.

There is some truth to those contentions: Except during the 1980s, the Communist leadership has invariably put investment before consumption. During the twenty years from 1956 through 1976, high rates of investment were made possible only by curbing consumption to a level that, in the rural areas, was not very much above subsistence.[22] But there is more to the story. Elements other than the mere curbing of consumption contributed to the high growth rates. Most important was that the regime initiated far-reaching reforms in industry and agriculture that made economic surpluses available for investment. The surpluses had previously accrued to private landowners and capitalists. At the same time the reforms increased productivity, especially in agriculture. Several analysts have pointed out that the lack of such basic reforms is responsible for a large, unrealized growth potential in Indian agriculture.[23] It is a main thesis in Barrington Moore's contribution that big landowners and moneylenders in India appropriate a large part of the agrarian surplus and spend it unproductively.[24] A number of scholars have echoed that opinion in more recent analyses, and it is a fact that the taxation of agricultural income in India has been extremely low, yielding only 1 percent of total tax proceeds in 1980–1981.[25] The strategy of the Green Revolution adopted in some areas of India in the mid-1960s aimed at increasing pro-

TABLE 3.1   Economic Growth in China and India

Indicators	China	India
GNP per capita, 1989 (dollars)	330	340
Real GDP per capita, 1993 (PPP$)[a]	2,330	1,240
Annual growth rate, GDP per capita (%)		
1965–1980	6.9	3.6
1980–1990	10.2	5.8
1990–1994	12.9	3.8
Industrial growth (% per annum)		
1950–1980[b]	12.1	5.5
1980–1990	11.1	7.1
1990–1994	18.8	3.2
Agricultural growth (% per annum)		
1950–1980[c]	3.1	2.3
1980–1990	5.9	3.1
1990–1994	4.1	2.9

[a]PPP (purchasing power parities): An attempt to measure real GDP in terms of domestic purchasing powers of currencies, thereby avoiding the distortions of official exchange rates.

[b]Figures for China are for 1953–1982; those for India are for 1956–1979.

[c]Figures for China are for 1952–1977.

Sources: United Nations Development Programme, *Human Development Report 1996* (New York: Oxford University Press, 1996); World Bank, *World Development Report 1996* (New York: Oxford University Press, 1996); Pranab Bardhan, *The Political Economy of Development in India* (Delhi: Oxford University Press, 1984); Jürgen Domes, *The Government and Politics of the PRC: A Time of Transition* (Boulder: Westview, 1985).

duction through the use of modern inputs, such as chemical fertilizers, pesticides, irrigation, and new crop varieties. The strategy has increased output where implemented, but it has not radically improved the overall growth rate in agriculture or paved the way for a substantially higher contribution from agriculture toward industrial growth.

Yet there are some less attractive elements in the Chinese growth record that must also be discussed. The power of the authoritarian regime to organize rapid economic growth also involves the power to commit horrible mistakes and even persevere in such mistakes, as occurred during the so-called Great Leap Forward, initiated in 1958, which was supposed to boost production to the extent that China could be among the highly industrialized countries in ten years' time. The Leap was a failure in industry and a disaster in agriculture; the production of food grain dropped in

1959 to the level of 1953. Only in 1978 did the per capita output of food grain reach the level of 1956.[26] In industry, output increased dramatically at first, but it then dropped at a similar speed in 1961–1962. Behind the rise in output was a complete lack of consideration for quality and for the cost of resources; behind the decline was an increasing organizational chaos and a misallocation of resources. In what can be seen only as an extreme arrogance of power, Mao Ze-dong, for reasons of personal pride, held onto the strategy of the Great Leap for some time even after it had proven catastrophically wrong.[27]

The Stalinist growth strategy that was employed in China must also be questioned from a more general perspective. It gave top priority to heavy industry while holding agriculture in an iron grip, allowing very few possibilities of increasing both investment and consumption in agriculture.[28] It is certainly this strategy that explains the substantial difference between Chinese industrial and agricultural rates of growth before 1980. It also helps explain why agricultural growth in China before 1980 was only slightly higher than in India (if, indeed, it was at all higher, given the uncertainty of the data).

The Stalinist strategy was changed after Mao's death. His successor, Deng Xiaoping, has pushed for reforms in industry and agriculture aimed at decentralization and a more prominent role for market forces. Such reforms are behind the much improved rates of growth in agriculture since 1980, but it has proven difficult to implement similar reforms in industry. China is currently in a phase of transition. Few people are interested in reverting to the old system of a highly centralized economic and political structure (with the exception, perhaps, of the groups in the state apparatus whose power hinges on that system), yet it has proven difficult to move toward a more decentralized, market-based system because the institutional preconditions are not present. These preconditions include a set of rules for conducting competition and for defining what is legal and illegal. Indeed, there is a lot of "official speculation" at the moment because these rules are not clear.[29] Also, there is no independent banking system for providing credit on commercial terms. And, perhaps most important, since the Tiananmen demonstrations in 1989 the leadership has been uncertain about how far it wishes to move down the road of reform. In short, the transformation toward another system is far from smooth and easy.

We have discussed economic growth in China and India. Let us now turn to the other aspect of economic development, welfare. There is no single best indicator for the level of welfare, but the United Nations Development Programme (UNDP) has in recent years published the *Human Development Report*, which ranks countries according to some of the best indicators. Drawing primarily on these data, Table 3.2 outlines the welfare achievements in China and India.

TABLE 3.2 Welfare in China and India

Indicators	China	India
Life expectancy at birth, 1993 (years)	68.6	60.7
Adult literacy rate, 1993 (%)	80.0	50.6
Under-age-five mortality rate, 1994 (per thousand)	43	119
Human Development index rank[a]	0.609	0.436

[a]The Human Development Index (HDI) is composed of three indicators: life expectancy, education, and income. For each indicator, a worldwide maximum (1) and minimum (0) are identified, and each country is then ranked according to its position. The combined average of the three positions is the HDI; the closer it is to 1, the better the ranking. See United Nations Development Programme, *Human Development Report 1991* (New York: Oxford University Press, 1991), p. 106.

Source: Figures from United Nations Development Programme, *Human Development Report 1996* (New York: Oxford University Press, 1996).

Even when we allow for some uncertainty in the data, there is no doubt about the general tendency: China has achieved a substantially higher level of welfare according to these indicators than has India. China's rating in the composite Human Development index is much better than India's. Note that the figures in the table are averages for the population as a whole. The situation for the poor is much worse. The percentage of the population living in **absolute poverty,** that is, at a minimum level of subsistence or below, is as high as 40 in India, and this percentage has basically remained unchanged since that country's independence. With a population increase from 360 million to more than 800 million between 1950 and 1988, there has been, of course, a dramatic increase in the number of very poor people. The corresponding percentage of the population living in absolute poverty in China is between 12 and 15.[30]

These data go squarely against the expectation that democratic regimes will give in to the electorate's demands for tangible benefits and will thus give priority to immediate welfare demands rather than to the long-term goals of investment and growth. The pertinent question is, of course, the following: Why has democratic India not done more for welfare?

Improved welfare for the masses has always received high priority in the development goals of Indian governments. But it is a long way from political rhetoric to actual welfare progress. First, good wishes must be translated into concrete political initiatives, and even in this early process we see a reduction in the rhetorical "welfare impulse." Second, to the extent that political measures are actually taken, there is a lack of implementation, especially in the rural sector. Welfare measures are perceived as a threat to the elite, who then fight to keep them from being carried out. Programs concerning the redistribution of land, tenancy regulations, minimum wage regulations, and the protection of the rural poor have all been subject to such resistance.[31] And when implementation does take place, there are often leakages in the delivery pipeline. Funds often end up in the hands of corrupt officials or middlemen; benefits are diverted at the end of the pipeline in favor of nontargeted, upper-income recipients.[32]

These are some of the mechanisms behind the lack of welfare progress in India. Their existence can be explained by looking at the structure of socioeconomic and political power that forms the basis of democracy in that country. Since independence, the Congress party has been dominated by three groups: the urban professionals, the bourgeoisie in industry and trade, and the rural landowning elite. It is, roughly speaking, the interests of these groups that have been looked after in the development policies of administrations led by the Congress party.[33]

Therefore, if we ask who have been the primary beneficiaries of the development policies conducted by the Indian state since independence, three groups emerge. First, there is the Indian bourgeoisie (or industrial capitalist class). With their control of a powerful nucleus of monopolistic undertakings, the bourgeoisie has enjoyed a protected domestic market and has benefited from a large public sector supplying the industrial infrastructure and other basic inputs at low prices; public financial institutions have provided a cheap source of finance, and the level of taxation has never constituted a serious burden.

Second, there are the rich farmers. They have benefited from price support for farm products and from a wide range of subsidized inputs (fertilizer, power, and water, for example). Moreover, the threat of land reform has been held in check, and there has been no significant taxation of agricultural income and wealth.

The third group is the bureaucracy, that is, the professionals and white-collar workers in the public sector. The benefits to this group have come from the substantial expansion of the public sector, partly by direct intervention in the economy in the form of public enterprises and partly through indirect controls; the bureaucracy has the power to grant licenses, subsidies, and other favors sought by the private sector.

In sum, Indian governments have presided over this coalition constituting roughly the top 20 percent of the population. It is a dominant coalition, and its position is reinforced because the government policies further, in the long run, the interests of its members.[34] The development policies of the state have never significantly been outside of the orbit of what is acceptable to the dominant coalition. The mass of poor people is too unorganized, divided, and politically weak to radically change this state of affairs.

Why, then, is there a much better welfare situation in China, in spite of an authoritarian government pushing economic growth? On the one hand, the reforms in agriculture promoted not only growth but also welfare. According to one estimate, the poorest fifth of the rural households increased its share of the overall income from 6 to 11 percent as a consequence of the agrarian reform.[35] On the other hand, a number of measures were taken that were aimed directly at welfare improvement. Three areas stand out in this respect, namely health, education, and public distribution systems. The average health situation in the country was substantially improved by the system of public health care erected in the 1950s and expanded to cover the rural areas during the 1960s. In addition to preventive care, the usual domain of public health care, this system also includes curative health care.[36] With regard to education, 93 percent of the relevant age-groups attended primary school in 1983, and even if more than one-third of the pupils from the rural areas drop out, the level of education has been considerably improved. Finally, the social security system in China includes the distribution of food through public channels that have extensive coverage.[37]

Yet there are also welfare elements in India's favor. Democratic India has avoided policy excesses, such as China's Great Leap Forward, that can lead to catastrophic situations. There has been no severe famine in India since independence; warning signals of such disasters are quickly relayed through a relatively free press, and the democratic government is prompted to take swift countermeasures. The situation is different in China. There was, for example, no free press to expose the failures of the Great Leap Forward and the severe famine that followed in its wake. The famine is estimated to have killed between 16.5 and 29.5 million people. At the same time, the more open political system in India has not provided protection against endemic undernutrition. Jean Drèze and Amartya Sen stated that "every eight years or so more people die in India because of its higher regular death rate than died in China in the gigantic famine of 1958–61. India seems to manage to fill its cupboard with more skeletons every eight years than China put there in its years of shame."[38]

In summary, the overall results in the growth and welfare aspects of economic development put authoritarian China ahead of democratic India. Radical reforms in China paved the way for economic development, which has provided a decent level of living for the large majority. The reforms could not have been implemented without a strong leadership bent on pushing such policies, perhaps even to the point of using coercion against opponents. But these radical reforms have also involved conflicts and mistaken policies that have led to human suffering and loss of life. Moreover, the other side of the strong, determined leadership is that it has promoted a system in which there is a blatant lack of basic civil and political rights.

In India the democratic government has, by and large, protected the basic civil and political rights of the people. Policy excesses have been avoided, as have human catastrophes such as large-scale famines. But democracy has also maintained a highly unequal social structure headed by a dominant elite whose members resist far-reaching change that would benefit the poor. The lack of progress on the welfare dimension in India has led to human suffering and loss of life, not through spectacular disasters like in China but through the quiet, continuous suffering of the 40 percent of the population who are in absolute poverty.

TYPES OF AUTHORITARIAN SYSTEMS

Comparison of the cases of India and China helped shed a more nuanced light on the theoretical debate over economic development outcomes of democratic and authoritarian regimes. Yet the debate obviously cannot be settled on the basis of one pair of cases. The comparison says nothing about the relationship between India/China and other examples of authoritarian and democratic regimes. Even if the India/China contrast does not give very high marks to Indian democracy, it is necessary to know more about different types of authoritarian and democratic systems and how India and China fit into this larger picture before further conclusions can be drawn. I shall argue in the sections that follow that China is indeed not very typical of the large group of authoritarian systems. China belongs, together with a few other countries, to a rather exclusive group of authoritarian developmentalist regimes that have been capable of promoting both economic growth and welfare. When we look at development outcomes, the large number of authoritarian systems belong to two less attractive groups: Either they push growth but not welfare or, even worse, they push neither. Regimes in this latter group do not have economic development as their main aim: Their ultimate goal is the enrichment of the elite, which controls the state. These three main types of authoritarian systems are outlined in Figure 3.2 and are further described in the sections that follow.

Authoritarian Developmentalist Regimes

The distinctive feature of an **authoritarian developmentalist regime** is its capability of promoting both growth and welfare. The government is reform oriented and enjoys a high degree of autonomy from vested elite interests. It controls a state apparatus with the bureaucratic, organizational capacity for promoting development and is run by a state elite that is ideologically committed toward boosting economic development in terms of growth as well as welfare. China is an example of a socialist authoritarian developmentalist regime. There is also a capitalist variety, with Taiwan

Regime type	Aspects of economic development		Country example
	Growth	Welfare	
Authoritarian developmentalist regime	+	+	Taiwan; China
Authoritarian growth regime	+	−	Brazil under military rule
Authoritarian state elite enrich- ment regime	−	−	Zaire under Mobutu

FIGURE 3.2   Types of authoritarian systems and their consequences for economic development

being an example. Even if they are often seen as opposites, Taiwan and China have several traits in common in addition to their authoritarian political systems. Taiwan, like China, pushed economic development through radical agrarian reform and the transfer of economic surplus from agriculture to industry. As in China, there has been a high degree of state involvement in the economy.

But the countries also have a number of dissimilar characteristics, some of which account for the fact that Taiwan has in several respects been more successful than its socialist counterpart.[39] First, the starting point experiences of the countries when they began to pursue economic development (around 1949) were different: China was engaged in a vicious civil war during the first half of the twentieth century; in the same period, orderly Japanese rule in Taiwan provided a basis for advances in economic development. Second, centralized planning like that in China has not been employed in Taiwan; the regime there has never attempted to monopolize economic power. The path taken by Taiwan more closely resembles the Japanese model, with a combination of market forces and private property and with heavy state guidance of the market, than the Chinese model. Taiwan seems to have struck a sound balance between the stagnation problems of "too much state" and the ultraliberalism of uncontrolled market forces that do not automatically serve the goals of economic development. Third, Taiwan has experienced a smooth process of growth and productivity increases in both agriculture, with its system of family farms, and industry, with its emphasis on light, labor-intensive manufacturing supported by public enterprises. In this process of economic reform, Taiwan has not experienced the severe setbacks due to policy failures that characterize China. The entire process has been supported by significant economic aid from the United States. China, conversely, imitated a Stalinist model of industrial growth, which overemphasized heavy industry and left very little room for growth in light industry and agriculture. It followed this policy until the late 1970s. In addition, China was internationally isolated for a long period, and its ties with the former Soviet Union during the 1950s did not yield much economic assistance compared to what Taiwan received from the United States.

Yet what must be stressed here is the basic similarity of China and Taiwan as members of the category of authoritarian developmentalist regimes. There are only a few other candidates for this type of authoritarian regime. The most obvious one is South Korea under authoritarian rule. North Korea was considered a socialist developmentalist regime in the 1960s and 1970s, but it has faltered due to political and economic mismanagement.[40] There are also a few borderline cases that share some of the features of authoritarian developmentalist regimes; examples are Singapore on the capitalist side and Cuba on the socialist side.

Authoritarian Growth Regimes

The second major type of authoritarian regime is the **authoritarian growth regime,** an elite-dominated government that promotes economic growth but not welfare. Brazil during military rule, from 1964 until the present period of redemocratization, is a good example of this form of rule. As an authoritarian growth regime, Brazil exhibited the following characteristics: It pursued economic growth objectives with the aim of building a strong national economy (which, in turn, could provide the basis for a strong military power), and it respected the long-term interests (but not necessarily the immediate interests) of the dominant social forces while it looked to the workers and peasants of the poor majority for the economic surplus needed to get growth under way.

The Brazilian regime was thus an explicitly elite-oriented model of development. It rested on an alliance between local private capital, state enterprises, and transnational corporations. The elite orientation of the model applies to the supply side of development (for the emphasis was on consumer durables) as well as to the demand side (for industrialization was capital intensive, with most benefits going to a small layer of skilled and white-collar employees and workers). The poor majority did not really benefit from the growth process; many had urgent needs in the areas of basic health, housing, education, and gainful employment.[41] Redistributive reform measures, including agrarian reform, could have helped push the welfare dimension of economic development, but what the regime undertook, especially in its early years, was exactly the opposite kind of redistribution. After having cut off popular organizations from political influence, the regime dramatically reduced real wages and took other measures that led to a substantial income concentration favoring the richest 20 percent of the population.[42]

The military regimes that imposed authoritarian rule in Uruguay, Chile, and Argentina in the early and mid-1970s attempted to implement models of economic growth with similar features. However, they were less successful than the Brazilian regime with regard to economic growth. In contrast to Brazil, these countries opened their economies to external shocks through the pursuit of ultraliberal economic policies, which, before corrective measures were taken, led to deindustrialization—that is, toward a dismantling of the existing industrial base.[43] Even so, these cases have a basic feature in common: The authoritarian regimes attempted to one-sidedly pursue economic growth in an alliance with elite interests.

Authoritarian State Elite Enrichment Regimes

The final major type of authoritarian rule, the **authoritarian state elite enrichment** (ASEE) **regime,** promotes neither growth nor welfare; its main aim is rather the enrichment of the elite, which controls the state. It is often based on autocratic rule by a supreme leader. Although the leader's actions may not make sense when judged by the standards of formal development goals set up by the regime, they are perfectly understandable through the lenses of patronage and clientelistic politics. It is clear that several African regimes, with their systems of personal rule as described in Chapter 2, are candidates for this category of authoritarianism. One observer has described the system as one of clan politics: "The clan is a political faction, operating within the institutions of the state and the governing party; it exists above all to promote the interests of its members . . . and its first unifying principle is the prospect of the material rewards of political success: loot is the clan's totem."[44]

The surplus that comes into the hands of the leadership through its control of the state is distributed among the clan or a coalition of clans, which in turn provide political support for the leader. It is not, of course, an equal pattern of distribution; the lion's share of the benefits accrues to the supreme leader and a small elite around him. There is no clear distinction between politicians and civil servants; the latter are actively involved in efforts to gain personal advantage from their public posts.

Thus, despite official claims to the contrary, the ruling elite takes no real interest in economic development, be it in terms of growth or welfare. The main aim of the regime is self-enrichment. Attainment of this goal requires an act of balancing against potential opponents (who are paid off or held down by force) and, as mentioned, also requires the distribution of spoils. Both may have side effects in terms of promoting either welfare or growth, but, again, this outcome is not the main aim.

Zaire (now Congo) under Mobutu may be the clearest example of an ASEE regime.[45] The inner circle of the Mobutu clan consisted of a few hundred people, Mobutu's "fraternity." The lucrative positions in the state, diplomatic corps, party, army, secret police, and the Presidency were reserved for clan members.[46] They directly claimed some 20 percent of the national budget, and their income was complemented through smuggling (diamonds and gold) and private sales of copper. Mobutu himself had a personal share in all foreign undertakings operating in Zaire, and his family controlled 60 percent of the domestic trade net. He has accumulated enormous wealth and is recognized to be one of the three richest people in the world.

Hence, the defining characteristic of the ASEE regime is simply that the elite who control the state are preoccupied with enriching themselves. Other examples from Africa that fit this description are the Central African Republic under Jean Bedel Bokassa and Uganda under Idi Amin. Examples of authoritarian regimes outside Africa that are also candidates for the ASEE category are Haiti under François and Jean-Claude Duvalier (Papa and Baby Doc), Nicaragua under Somoza, and Paraguay under Alfredo Stroessner.

*   *   *

What can be learned from this typology of authoritarian regimes? First, it is not possible to generalize across authoritarian systems in terms of their capacities for promoting economic development. Different authoritarian regimes vary greatly in this respect. In this chapter, we described three main categories of authoritarian systems: the authoritarian developmentalist regimes, capable of promoting both growth and welfare; the authoritarian growth regimes, which give priority to economic growth; and the ASEE regimes, which promote neither growth nor welfare. Second, authoritarianism does not automatically generate economic growth, order, and stability, as those advocating a trade-off between democracy and economic development contend. The authoritarian growth regime is perhaps the type closest to the mainstream view of authoritarian regimes held by those advocating the trade-off. Under this system, economic growth is promoted at the expense of the welfare of the majority of the population. Although proponents of this system seem to think that a long phase of growth can provide a good basis for improving welfare at a later stage, the case of authoritarian Brazil appears to demonstrate the opposite. In that country, a number of impediments prevented the expected trickle-down effect from making itself felt on a scale at which it could significantly contribute to welfare improvement.[47] One important reason was the specific elite orientation of the growth process.

Finally, the typology sets the trade-off debate in a new light by emphasizing the diversity of authoritarian regimes. If we examine the ASEE regime in Zaire, we find that authoritarianism is definitely worse for economic development than its rumor; if we study the authoritarian developmentalist regime in Taiwan, we find that authoritarianism is much better for economic development than its rumor.

Against this background, and with the knowledge that authoritarian developmentalist systems of the Taiwan type are few and far between, it is easy to reject the argument that there is a trade-off between democracy and economic development on the ground that most authoritarian systems do not fare any better than democracies in the area of development. And then there is no reason to sacrifice the rights and liberties associated with democracy. Before we draw final conclusions, however, let us take a closer look at different types of democracies.

TYPES OF DEMOCRATIC SYSTEMS

It is more difficult to create a typology of democratic systems than one of authoritarian systems simply because there are very few relatively stable democracies in the developing world. If we do not count very small countries with populations of less than one million, only Costa Rica (with a population of three million) has been a stable democracy for as long as India. Venezuela and Colombia come close to a similar stability. Yet there is a common denominator between these stable cases and the majority of the current transitions discussed in Chapter 2 that is significant for their economic development outlooks. They are all **elite-dominated democracies** (systems in which traditional rulers remain in control, even if pressured from below, and successfully use strategies of either compromise or force—or some mix of the two—to retain at least part of their power).

Elite-Dominated Democracies

Indian democracy, in the vein of the current transitions toward democracy, was achieved by an elite-dominated coalition with three main groups: the urban professionals, who founded the Congress movement in 1885; the Indian business community in trade and industry; and the rural landowning elite. The masses of poor peasants supported the elite coalition's struggle for independence and democracy; they rallied behind Gandhi as the great leading figure who would be instrumental in welding this alliance between elite groups and the poor masses. Yet the support of the poor peasants did not really upset the rural elite. Gandhi's vision of the future of the Indian villages included no threat to their position, and it was the rural elite, not the landless peasants, who controlled the Congress organization at the local level.[48]

We have already seen that the continued elite dominance in the Indian democracy shaped and set the limits of what could be achieved in terms of economic development. The process of economic development has mainly served the interests of the elite groups in the dominant coalition. The respect for elite interests has impeded the capacity of Indian democracy to mobilize resources for economic growth and welfare improvement through basic agrarian and other reforms.

In Chapter 2, the majority of the current transitions toward democracy were characterized as transitions from above—that is, elite-dominated transitions. We saw the fears expressed there that the regimes may become frozen democracies, which is Terry Lynn Karl's term for restricted elite-dominated democracies that are unwilling to transgress the narrow limitations imposed on them by the elite factions who engineered the transitions to democracy in the first place. They are unwilling to carry out substantive reforms that address the lot of the poor citizens. Against the background of the Indian experience with some forty years of elite-dominated democracy, such fears are well founded; there has been economic development in India both in terms of growth and welfare, but as a whole the process has offered much too little to the mass of poor people.

But it is important to emphasize another point raised in Chapter 2: Democracy introduces a degree of uncertainty in the political process. It opens channels for popular pressure on the rulers. Even elite-dominated democracies may be pushed in the direction of more effective reform measures, as can be seen in the following case study of Costa Rica.

In Costa Rica, democracy was based on political pacts between elite factions. The three main groups in the dominant coalition in Costa Rica are the elites in export agriculture and in industry (including foreign investors) and the members of the state bureaucracy.[49] They shared the benefits of a development model that is based on export agriculture and promotes industrialization and a strong role for the state in certain areas. Thus, export agriculture has received constant government support, the level of taxation has been quite modest, and the agrarian reform measures have been no threat. Although industrialists have had to accept that agriculture could not be restructured according to the specific needs of industrialization, industry has received ample support in terms of external protection, low tariffs for inputs, tax exemptions, and comprehensive infrastructural support from the public sector. The bureaucracy has grown stronger through the rapid expansion of a great variety of institutions in the public sector, which has provided a solid basis from which further benefits could be negotiated from the state.

In this sense, Costa Rican democracy may be seen as "a masked hegemony of competing elites who have explicitly agreed to respect one another's interests."[50] Policies are based on a balance between different elites respecting one another's basic interests. Thus, welfare programs have been kept within limits acceptable to the dominant interests. Radical social programs of structural change have been avoided, as have economic policies that could pose a serious threat to any elite faction. As a result, welfare improvements in Costa Rica rest on the shaky basis of an agrarian export economy saddled with a heavy (and increasing) foreign debt.

Yet, within these limitations, the dominant coalitions in Costa Rica have supported governments that have promoted substantial welfare programs. As shown in Table 3.3, the overall achievements of the country are fairly impressive with respect to welfare, whereas the economic growth achievements have been more ordinary, especially during the crisis period in the 1980s. It should be noted that the average figures given in Table 3.3 conceal the existence of a fairly large group of people at the bottom of the ladder that has made much less progress. Although there are very few at the level of actual starvation, one estimate from 1977 put the share of the population living at the subsistence level at 17 percent.[51] Most of these people belong to the rural landless or the urban populations from the city slums. The economic crisis of the 1980s has meant a setback for the majority of the population. As early as 1982, real wages were back at the level of 1970 and cutbacks in state expenditure had hit several social programs.

Still, the elite-dominated democracy of Costa Rica has fared relatively well in terms of welfare. Several elements go into explaining this achievement. First, the nature of elite rule in Costa Rica during the nineteenth and early twentieth centuries was different from that in most other countries in Latin America. Costa Rica did not have a system with Indians and slaves under the control of a rural elite; there was an independent peasantry, and the rural working class was free from feudal ties binding them to rural patrons. Second, the dominant stratum of coffee barons supported liberal values of religious freedom, freedom of the press, and the promotion of public education. A law for free, compulsory education was passed in 1884, and the educational level of the population combined with open public debate paved the way for the formation of a variety of groups and associations that fed demands into the political system.[52] Third, the democracy established after 1948 has a reputation for fair and honest elections in a political system geared toward negotiation and compromise. In dramatic contrast to its Central American neighbors, Costa Rica disbanded its army in 1949.

The case of Costa Rica demonstrates that elite-dominated democracies need not fare as poorly as, for example, India has fared in welfare terms.

TABLE 3.3   Welfare and Growth in Costa Rica

Life expectancy at birth, 1993 (years)	76.4
Adult literacy rate, 1993 (%)	94.5
Human Development index rank[a]	0.884
Real GDP per capita, 1993 (PPP$)[b]	5,680
Annual growth rate, GNP per capita (%)	
1965–1980	3.3
1980–1993	1.1

[a]The Human Development Index (HDI) is composed of three indicators: life expectancy, education, and income. For each indicator, a worldwide maximum (1) and minimum (0) are identified, and each country is then ranked according to its position. The combined average of the three positions is the HDI; the closer it is to 1, the better the ranking. See United Nations Development Programme, *Human Development Report 1991* (New York: Oxford University Press, 1991), p. 106.

[b]PPP (purchasing power parities): An attempt to measure real GDP in terms of domestic purchasing powers of currencies, thereby avoiding the distortions of official exchange rates.

Source: Figures from United Nations Development Programme, *Human Development Report 1996* (New York: Oxford University Press, 1996).

They are capable of transforming toward a higher degree of responsiveness to mass demands. But the political background of Costa Rica contains some rather unique features, which are hard to find in other elite-dominated democracies, that allowed it to move in this direction. The egalitarian values of the dominant coalition led to a social and political environment that was conducive to the organization of popular forces at an early stage. These elements provided the basis for welfare policies and for the formation of "a system of stable liberal democracy without parallel in Latin America."[53]

As shown by this case study, elite-dominated democracies can address welfare issues. Unfortunately, there are few elite-dominated democracies that have conditions similar to those that were instrumental for bringing this result about in Costa Rica.

Mass-Dominated Democracies

Mass-dominated democracies are systems in which mass actors have gained the upper hand over traditional ruling classes. They push for reforms from below, attacking the power and privilege of the elites. A prominent example of this system of rule is the Unidad Popular (Popular Unity) government under Salvador Allende in Chile between 1970 and 1973. The government was elected on a program promising massive improvement for low-income and poor groups in terms of wage and salary increases and better social and housing conditions. It also promoted measures for making the economy more effective; policies would be geared to faster growth and increased popular control. It implemented policies for the redistribution of land through agrarian reform and for the nationalization of the mineral sector, something that it also foresaw for the largest enterprises in the private sector.[54]

Although successful in its first year in power, the Unidad Popular faced rapidly growing resistance from landowners, industrialists, and the middle sectors. A process of radicalization took place in which an increasingly united opposition faced a government that was divided internally over whether it should radically confront or moderately accommodate its political adversaries. It was this situation that in 1973 culminated in the military coup led by Augusto Pinochet. This example underlines the fragility of mass-dominated democracies; they easily lead toward hostile confrontation, which may then result in a return to authoritarian rule.

The fate of the Unidad Popular and other mass-dominated democracies in Latin America has led to rather pessimistic conclusions regarding the future possibilities for such systems in the region, as we saw in Chapter 2. Set in a broader perspective, the picture may be a bit brighter. It should be possible for mass-dominated democracies to proceed more cautiously along the road of reform than did the Unidad Popular, for example, and thereby avoid the kind of all-encompassing showdown that took place in Chile. A government that has been successful in this way is the Left Front rule in West Bengal, India, which came to power in 1977.[55] At the same time, democracies have transformative capacities. The development of most West European democracies since the nineteenth century can be seen as a process beginning with elite-dominated systems and then gradually transforming toward more mass-dominated systems. The latter, in turn, are responsible for the welfare states built since the 1930s. The process of gradual transformation paved the way for elite acceptance of social reforms and equity policies.

*   *   *

From the examples given we can see that the economic development prospects of democratic systems, especially concerning the likelihood of improvements for the underprivileged, depend on the nature of the ruling coalitions behind the democracies. Highly restricted, elite-dominated democracies may be virtually "frozen" in that their room for maneuver in addressing welfare issues and also in promoting resources for economic growth is set within the very narrow limits of continued support for the status quo. If, as was argued earlier, most of the current transitions toward democracy are from above (that is, elite-dominated), the pessimistic projection that many of the current transitions will develop into frozen democracies remains rather convincing.

Mass-dominated democracies are not frozen in this way. They contain the potential for substantial reform going against vested elite interests. But such reform may lead to confrontation with elite forces and to the subsequent undermining of democracy itself.

Yet there is a space between these extremes where relatively stable democracy and economic progress can go hand in hand. The elite-dominated systems are not necessarily locked in their frozen positions forever. They have transformative capacities that may lead to a higher responsiveness to popular demands. The Scandinavian welfare states are examples of countries that have undertaken this transformation.

ECONOMIC PERFORMANCE IN THE CURRENT DEMOCRATIC TRANSITIONS

The previous reflections have focused on the more long-term economic consequences of elite-dominated and mass-dominated democracies. But most of the current democratic transitions have now conducted economic policies for five or more years. What can we say about their economic policy performances during that time?

A recent research project has addressed this question through an analysis of twelve middle-income countries: in Latin America—Argentina, Bolivia, Brazil, Chile, Peru, Mexico, and Uruguay; and in Asia—South Korea, Taiwan, the Philippines, Thailand, and Turkey.[56] Some of these countries have been relatively successful in their economic policy—they have achieved economic stability and created good conditions for economic growth. Others have been much less successful. Given the fact that all of these countries are, in varying degrees, elite-dominated democracies, that factor alone cannot explain the differences in their economic policy performances. What, then, are the main conditions influencing economic policy performance in the short term?

The study by Haggard and Kaufman singles out two types of structural factors—one economic and the other political—that help answer that question. The economic factor considers the presence or absence of economic crisis at the time of democratic takeover; the political factor considers a country's ability to organize stable political rule.

Some of the new democracies examined in this study came to power amid severe economic crisis, characterized by high inflation and macroeconomic instability. Such was the case in Argentina, Brazil, Bolivia, Peru, and Uruguay. Economic crisis creates a difficult situation for new, democratic administrations. These administrations must deal with highly adverse economic conditions; there is, however, a strong public expectation that a democratic regime will substantially improve conditions and that economic benefits will quickly flow from democratization. This dilemma creates an incentive to move toward a form of "soft authoritarianism," with a strong executive and a weak parliament, as in Peru, where President Fujimori closed congress and assumed dictatorial power in 1992. Yet this has not been the general pattern. In the other countries examined, policies of adjustment and macroeconomic stability were eventually implemented under democratic conditions; given the harsh economic conditions, the new democracies performed fairly well. "Democratization per se cannot, therefore, be considered the culprit for policy failures . . . regime change may have only a slight effect on policy, or even provide opportunities for new reform initiatives."[57]

In new democracies free from economic crisis (Thailand, South Korea, Chile, and Turkey), there has been a high degree of continuity in economic policy. Democratic administrations have essentially carried on the economic policy of their authoritarian predecessors. Although such policies may favor economic stability and growth in the short term, they also contain an inherent weakness of favoring those groups in the population that supported the authoritarian regime. As a result, the weaker and poorer groups that suffered most under authoritarianism continue to be disadvantaged under democracy. The consequence may be increasing polarization, with negative effects on democracy—a variant of the elite-dominated, frozen democracy identified earlier.

As described above, the political factor influencing economic policy performance in new democracies is the ability to organize stable political rule. This ability depends on political institutions, especially on the existence of a political party system that is not too fragmented or polarized (fragmentation increases with the number of competing parties; polarization increases with growing ideological distance among parties). In the cases examined by Haggard and Kaufman, "fragmented and polarized party systems have posed major impediments to sustained implementation of reform."[58]

Successful economic policy performance, then, depends heavily on a robust party system that is not seriously fragmented or polarized. Especially in Latin America (Uruguay is an exception), the lack of such a party system has led to "profound policy failures."[59] The worst cases of fragmentation and polarization of the party system in new democracies, however, are outside of the universe of cases examined by Haggard and Kaufman: They are in sub-Saharan Africa and Eastern Europe, including Russia.

There is a connection, of course, between the short-term economic policy performance of new democracies discussed here and the long-term economic performance discussed earlier. New democracies capable of weathering severe economic crisis and able to formulate and implement sound economic policies leading to stability and growth will also have the best possibilities for addressing welfare issues and thus for improving conditions for large groups of poor. Such democracies are also most likely to consolidate democratic rule and avoid authoritarian regress.

In sum, this section has demonstrated how the economic and political legacy of some new democracies better prepare these democracies for the transformation from frozen to more broadly responsive systems that can offer both political participation and social and economic benefits to the large majority. It must also be emphasized, however, that such a transformation has not yet taken place, not even in those countries in which the preconditions are favorable.

DEMOCRACY AND
ECONOMIC DEVELOPMENT IN PERSPECTIVE

Drawing on the typologies of authoritarian and democratic systems presented in this chapter and the comparative considerations discussed, we can now derive some general conclusions regarding the possible trade-off between democracy, on the one hand, and economic development, on the other. First, there is not a one-to-one relationship between the form of regime (democratic or authoritarian) and development outcomes for the simple reason that different types of democratic and authoritarian regimes have different development capacities. If we compare the elite-dominated type of democracy with the authoritarian developmentalist regime, as was done in the India/China comparison, it is possible to argue that there is a trade-off between democracy and development because the authoritarian developmentalist regime performs better in development than the elite-dominated democracy does. This conclusion, however, is not strong enough to support the notion of a *general* trade-off between democracy and development; other types of authoritarian systems perform worse in economic development than the authoritarian developmentalist ones, and the democratic regimes might come out on top in comparisons with those systems.

Second, with regard to the relatively few authoritarian developmentalist systems that perform well in economic development, we need to demonstrate in precise terms how and to what extent the suspension of civil and political rights can be justified in order to promote economic development. For example, although it may well be that socialist authoritarianism in China provided the regime with a freedom of maneuver that paved the way for the radical redistribution of land to the benefit of the rural masses, the development benefits hardly justify a blanket trade-off between development and all types of civil and political rights. As one scholar has noted, such violations as "torture, disappearances, and arbitrary executions can almost always be eliminated with no costs to development; rights to nationality and to equality before the law would also seem to have very low development costs; due process is likely to be a bit more costly, but the burden seems bearable. . . . In other words, tradeoffs of civil and political rights must be selective, flexible, and rather specific if they are to be justified at all."[60] Therefore, even in those cases where the trade-off seems justified, it is necessary to examine which rights really require suspension in order to promote development.

We have stated that the theory of a general trade-off between democracy and development must be rejected. Yet rejection of that statement does not mean that democracy and economic development automatically go hand in hand, mutually reinforcing each other. Behind the rejected trade-off are other, equally serious dilemmas. First, there seem to be a fairly large number of both authoritarian *and* democratic systems that, for different reasons, do not perform well in terms of economic development. The ASEE regimes and the elite-oriented authoritarian growth regimes, together with the elite-dominated frozen democracies, seem to hold out few promises for a process of economic development that will benefit the large masses of poor people.

Second, with regard to the main types of democracies, there seems to be a trade-off between stability, on the one hand, and the capacity for promoting rapid economic development, on the other. The elite-dominated democracies by far hold the best prospects for stability, as the Latin American experiences illustrate; at the same time, elite dominance can often mean support for the status quo and little development progress. Mass-dominated democracies promise more rapid economic advance through reforms attacking vested elite interests, but instability and reversion to authoritarianism may be the result. It was argued earlier that there is a space between these extremes where democracy and economic development can go hand in hand. Democracies have transformative capacities, as the case of Costa Rica demonstrates; but only some of the present transitions toward democracy hold the promise of being able to strike the necessary balance between democratic stability and economic development.

DEMOCRACY AND HUMAN RIGHTS

Development is concerned not only with progress in material terms (food, housing, health service, education, and so forth); it also involves a nonmaterial aspect that has to do with human freedom, identity, and security.[61] The latter can be gathered under the umbrella of human rights, especially civil and political human rights.[62] They include such elements as the prohibition of torture, the right to a fair trial and to equal protection under the law, freedom from arbitrary arrest, freedom of movement and residence, and freedom of thought, conscience, and religion.

What is the relationship between democracy and human rights? Does democracy promote human rights? On first impression, the answers seem to be straightforward. The definition of political democracy given in Chapter 1 involved civil and political rights: freedom of expression, freedom of the press, freedom of association, and the right of political participation. If civil and political rights are part of the definition of democracy itself, then democracies, one would think, must promote those rights. Democracies may not always promote, for example, economic development, but at least they provide for basic civil and political rights.

One scholar has tried to sort out the relationship between political democracy as measured by Freedom House and the pattern of human rights violations based on information from the U.S. State Department. As shown in Table 3.4, the democratic ("free") systems respect rights to a much higher degree than the authoritarian ("not free") systems.

However, further scrutiny reveals problems at two points. First, the relationship between democracy and the promotion of human rights is not perfect. Many democracies promote the basic political freedoms associated with democracy while they violate other human rights. Such violations are monitored by Amnesty International. In recent years even the long-standing and consolidated democracy of Denmark has been mentioned in Amnesty's report on human rights violations (the case in question had to do with the state's violation of the right to humane treatment under detention for some visitors from developing countries). Therefore, if rights are defined in a very broad sense, even the most democratic countries might not fully provide all of them. This point is supported by data in the Human Freedom index constructed by United Nations Development Programme.[63] The index lists forty rights and freedoms, including social and economic equality for ethnic minorities, freedom for independent newspapers and book publishing, and freedom from capital punishment. It then ranks countries according to the extent to which they respect these forty different rights. None of the eighty-eight countries listed in 1985 observed all of the freedoms. Sweden and Denmark topped the list, with thirty-eight out of forty freedoms guaranteed to their people. They were followed by the Netherlands with thirty-seven, and Finland, New Zealand, and Austria with thirty-six. Some democracies had rather low scores, such as India (fourteen), Colombia (fourteen), Israel (nineteen), Spain (twenty-six), and Italy (twenty-nine). At the bottom of the list were Iraq (zero!), Libya (one), and China (two). Yet, although this information may cast some democracies in an unfavorable light, it does not seem to break the general rule that democracies show higher respect for

TABLE 3.4   Democracy and Human Rights, 1990: Percentage of States Committing Selected Violations

Human Rights Violations	Not Free	Free
Summary executions	11	2
Disappearances	56	20
Massacres	24	3
Arbitrary arrest	88	31
No fair or decent trial	86	23
Torture	84	25

Source: Based on Berto Jongman, "Why Some States Kill and Torture While Others Do Not," PIOOM Newsletter and Progress Report 3, no. 1 (1991): 9.

human rights than do authoritarian systems, even if this respect may not be complete.

But there is a second problem with the contention that democracy and human rights are two sides of the same coin. It has to do with the incompleteness of many of the transitions toward democracy. Many regimes are still restricted democracies in which there is also insufficient respect for civil and political rights.

In addition, some transitions provoke turbulence and instability, which can also have negative effects for human rights. In this context one scholar has emphasized that not only authoritarian rule but also the breakdown of authority involves major human rights violations.[64] The breakdown of authority means the weakening of the authority of a government (democratic or authoritarian) to the point that it is on the verge of losing power or to the point that it must employ harsh means to hold on to power.[65] Thus, a high violation of human rights can be seen in crisis-ridden transitions toward democracy, where weak civilian goverments are struggling to stay in authority. In other words, the political freedoms (competition, participation) may indicate fairly democratic conditions, but the breakdown of authority leads to a high degree of human rights violation. Many countries fall into this category, including Colombia, El Salvador, Paraguay, Peru, Bulgaria, Nicaragua, Panama, the Philippines, Turkey, and Sri Lanka.

In summary, democracies as a rule give higher respect to human rights in general than authoritarian regimes do. When countries are viewed against a very comprehensive list of human rights, it appears that many democracies violate some of them. Furthermore, transitions toward democracy may lead to breakdowns of authority, which can result in even higher human rights violations than would be the case under stable authoritarian conditions. Thus, stable and consolidated democracy correlates with a high respect for human rights in general, but the move toward democracy and the early phases of democratic opening that characterize the majority of the current transitions can produce situations with a high degree of human rights violation.

CONCLUSION

This chapter opened by asking whether democracy is really worth the trouble and by asking if it paves the way for improvements in spheres of life other than those narrowly connected with political freedoms. A number of reasons were given for an affirmative answer to both questions. Not only is democracy a value in itself, but it helps promote other civil and political rights. Furthermore, although democracies may not invariably perform better than authoritarian systems in terms of economic development, the notion of a general trade-off between democracy and development was rejected. Most of the authoritarian systems are oppressive, and they are also poor performers in terms of economic development.

At the same time, transitions toward democracy do not guarantee a promised land of rapid economic development and a vastly improved human rights situation. The elite-dominated frozen democracies seem to hold out few promises for a process of economic development that would benefit the large groups of poor people. The transitions themselves can lead to situations of instability and the breakdown of authority that involve higher human rights violation than before. The promise of democracy is not that of automatic improvement in areas of life that are not narrowly connected with political freedoms; it is the creation of a window of opportunity, a political framework where groups struggling for development and human rights have better possibilities than before for organizing and expressing their demands. Democracy offers the opportunities; it does not offer guarantees of success.

FOUR

□   □   □

International Consequences
of Democracy:
Peace and Cooperation?

Will the spread of democracy mean the end of war? Can we look forward
to a more peaceful world focused on cooperation toward mutual gain instead of conflict and violence? This chapter examines the consequences
for international relations of the spread of democracy. Democracy is again
treated as the independent variable; the aim is to discover its effects on relations between states and on the nature of the international system.

The scholarly debate contains widely diverging views. One school of
thought expects profoundly positive consequences from the spread of
democracy; another completely rejects the importance of democracy for
international relations. We shall see that these seemingly contrasting
views are not entirely incompatible, but first the main arguments in the
theoretical debate must be presented.

THE DEBATE ON DEMOCRACY AND PEACE

The argument that democracy is an important force for peace has as its
most forceful advocate the German philosopher Immanuel Kant. In his essay "Perpetual Peace," which was published in 1795, Kant developed his
argument in several stages.[1] First, he pointed to a natural tendency for
states to organize in the form of liberal republics because that system of rule
bestows legitimacy on the political leaders and promotes popular support
for the state, making it well suited to face foreign threats. In other words,
states not organized as liberal republics will tend to be unsuccessful.

A "liberal republic" corresponds roughly to what is called a political
democracy in this book. Thus, the establishment of democracies in the

world is a natural tendency according to Kant, although there may be many setbacks. Once established, democracies will lead to peaceful relations because democratic governments are controlled by the citizens and therefore will not enter into violent conflict that may subject the citizens to bloodshed and war. In Kant's words,

> If the consent of the citizens is required in order to decide that war should be declared . . . nothing is more natural than that they would be very cautious in commencing such a poor game, decreeing for themselves all the calamities of war. Among the latter would be: having to fight, having to pay the costs of war from their own resources, having painfully to repair the devastation war leaves behind, and, to fill up the measure of evils, load themselves with heavy national debt that would embitter peace itself and that can never be liquidated on account of constant wars in the future.[2]

One of the great social scientists of the twentieth century, Joseph Schumpeter, has also supported the notion of peaceful democracies. His reasoning is similar to Kant's. Schumpeter has argued that imperialist expansion and war benefit only a minority of profiteers, arms producers, and members of the military establishment. Therefore, "no democracy would pursue a minority interest and tolerate the high costs of imperialism."[3]

There is some empirical support for these views. A study by R. J. Rummel looked at libertarian states (meaning those emphasizing political and economic freedom) and contrasted the involvement of these "free" states in conflict at or above the level of economic sanctions with that of "nonfree" and "partly free" states. The conclusion was that of the violence during the period 1976 to 1980, only 24 percent of the free states were involved, compared with 26 percent of the partly free and 61 percent of the nonfree states. In other words, the more libertarian a state, the less it is involved in foreign violence. Rummel further claimed that a number of previous studies support this conclusion.[4]

However, several recent studies have rejected the idea that democracies are more peaceful than other regimes. Melvin Small and J. David Singer studied wars between 1816 and 1965 and found no significant differences between democracies and other regimes in terms of frequency of war involvement. This conclusion was supported by Steve Chan in his study of wars between 1816 and 1980; it was also supported by Erich Weede's study of war involvement between 1960 and 1980. It should be noted that Rummel's study lends itself to criticism because it covers only the period 1976 to 1980. The studies based on longer periods of observation deserve more credibility. In addition, Rummel's way of surveying the literature can be criticized.[5] Indeed, there is overwhelming consensus among scholars that democracies have gone to war as often as have other types of regimes.

But the debate does not end there because the empirical studies have come up with a finding that revives the optimists' hopes for democracy as a road to peace. Although democracies are as war-prone as other types of regimes, democracies do not fight one another: *"Even though liberal states have become involved in numerous wars with nonliberal states, constitutionally secure liberal states have yet to engage in war with each other."*[6] The empirical investigations provide substantial support for this claim. The observation was first emphasized by Dean Babst in 1964, and it has been confirmed in numerous studies since then.[7] Indeed, one scholar has called the assertion that democracies do not fight each other "one of the strongest nontrivial or nontautological statements that can be made about international relations."[8]

This finding, then, is the basis of the present optimism among many scholars and policymakers. Their reasoning goes as follows: The number of democracies in the world has increased rapidly in recent years and democracies do not fight one another; therefore, we can look forward to a much more peaceful world with international relations characterized by cooperation instead of conflict. If their assertion is true, it seems that profound revision is also needed of the dominant theoretical paradigm in international relations, namely **realism.** (Realism, in this context, is a theoretical perspective on international relations that purports to analyze the world as it really is, not as it ought to be. According to this perspective, conflict in the real world is imminent due to forces inherent in human nature and due to the way the world's populations have chosen to organize in the form of independent, sovereign states that respect no authority outside or above themselves.) With realism, the major characteristic of the international system is the lack of authority above the sovereign nation-states, which is what makes the system an unsafe anarchy where states constantly have to fear violent conflict with other states. If we are to believe that democracies do not fight one another, then a substantial modification of the notion of anarchy leading to violent conflict is called for.

Before we move on with these issues, however, it is helpful to return to Kant. Kant was well aware that democracy would lead not to the total abolishment of war, but only to peace between democracies. His point of departure was outlined earlier: There are constitutional mechanisms in democracies that restrain them from going to war because of the burdens war imposes on the population. Yet these restraints are effective only in relations with other democracies. Why only there? Kant gave two reasons—one moral, the other economic. The moral reason has to do with the common values of legitimate rights held by democracies and with the mutual respect and understanding between democracies. These bonds lead to what Kant called a **pacific union,** which is not a signed treaty but a zone of peace based on the common moral foundation of the democra-

FIGURE 4.1 Elements of Kant's pacific union among democracies

cies (see Fig. 4.1). Peaceful ways of solving domestic conflicts are seen as morally superior to violent behavior, and this view is transferred to international relations between democracies. The beginning of cooperation starts a virtuous circle of increasing cooperation: "As culture grows and men gradually move towards greater agreement over their principles, [these agreed-upon principles] lead to mutual understanding and peace."[9] The transparency of democracies is important for the whole process. Freedom of expression and free communication help establish mutual understanding internationally and help assure that political representatives act in accordance with citizens' views domestically.

The economic reason is based on the benefits from international trade and investment. In the pacific union it is possible to focus on what Kant called "the spirit of commerce," the possibility for mutual gain for those involved in international economic cooperation. The development of economic interdependence that occurs when notions of autarky (self-sufficiency) are set aside and the pursuit of mutual economic gain is given priority, further strengthens the pacific union.

In sum, there are three elements behind Kant's claim that democracy leads to peace. The first is the mere existence of democracies, with their culture of peaceful conflict resolution. Second, the democracies hold common moral values, and the bonds they forge because of these values lead to the formation of a pacific union. Finally, the pacific union is strengthened through economic cooperation and interdependence. All three elements are necessary in order to make the connection between democracy and peace. But it is important to bear in mind that democracies continue to go to war with nondemocratic regimes, with whom they have no common moral foundation. Between the democracies themselves, peace is predicated upon the existence of a pacific union with ties of economic interdependence. These elements do not come about automatically; they are formed in a process in which the early results of cooperation lead to further cooperative efforts. There can be reversals, a backsliding toward the use of violence, warned Kant, but ultimately the pacific union will expand and provide perpetual peace among all democratic nations. As Kant has also argued for the victory of democracy as the superior form of state, it follows that in the end peace will prevail among all nations.

Such is the positive vision formulated by Kant. In order to evaluate its prospects in relation to the current processes of democratization, it is necessary to further examine each of the elements of Kant's vision in a contemporary context. We will look first at the domestic scene and then at international relations.

THE DOMESTIC SCENE:
FOREIGN POLICY IN DEMOCRACIES

Democracies show restraint in their relations with other democracies but not with nondemocratic regimes. Why the possible belligerence toward the latter? Although relations between the states within the pacific union are characterized by cooperation, outside the pacific union the power struggle between states for security, resources, and prestige continues; there, the realist picture of an international system characterized by anarchy applies. Democracies have reasons to be skeptical in their relations with governments that cannot claim to represent their peoples. As one observer has written, "Because nonliberal governments are in a state of aggression with their own people, their foreign relations become for liberal governments deeply suspect. In short, fellow liberals benefit from a presumption of amity; nonliberals suffer from a presumption of enmity."[10] War as the outcome of conflict is always a possibility under these circumstances.

Further, democratic regimes can go to war for crusade reasons—that is, in order to promote democratic values in new areas. In this sense, "The very constitutional restraint, shared commercial interests, and international respect for individual rights that promote peace among liberal societies can exacerbate conflicts in relations between liberal and nonliberal societies."[11] This view helps explain the liberal democratic vigilance toward nondemocratic areas, especially the self-imposed "white man's burden" of bringing civilized government and order to the colonies. Obviously, this view is very ethnocentric: Western civilization is seen as vastly superior to the "barbarian" ways of the indigenous peoples of the colonies; thus, it is only reasonable that the colonies are being subjected to Western leadership, if necessary by force. Later, the liberation movements of the colonies turned the argument against their Western masters: Self-government, so ran their claim, is a legitimate right according to democratic principles. This counterargument led many colonial masters to lose faith in their right to rule and provided an important impetus to the process of decolonization.[12]

Finally, it can be argued that democracy introduces an element of irrationality to foreign policy-making. Instead of using prudence in international relations, democracies may succumb to whims of public opinion or moods of possible belligerence or appeasement that may result in confused, unwise policies. Walter Lippmann argued that public opinion has forced governments "to be too late with too little, or too long with too much, too pacifist in peace and too bellicose in war, too neutralist or appeasing in negotiation or too transient."[13]

This irrationality in foreign policy-making introduces a dilemma in the way democracies conduct foreign affairs: The democratic framework of government is a cornerstone of the pacific union, but at the same time democracy can lead to imprudent, adventurous policies toward non-democratic regimes. Removing this irrationality from policy-making would seem to require an executive more unrestrained from the representative legislature than current executives are, but change in that direction would, in turn, threaten the basis for the pacific union. In other words, "completely resolving liberal dilemmas may not be possible without threatening liberal success."[14]

It is against the background of this dilemma that a long-standing debate is taking place about the proper amount of public influence on foreign policy in democracies. There are two main positions. On one side, there are those who agree with John Locke's argument that foreign policy should be left to the experts. He was supported in this view by Alexis de Tocqueville, who feared that foreign policy subjected to a democratic process would lead to poor results. A democracy, said Tocqueville in 1835, is "unable to regulate the details of an important undertaking, to persevere in a design, and to work out its execution in the presence of serious obstacles. It cannot combine its measures with secrecy, and will not await their consequences with patience."[15]

On the other side are supporters of the argument that a genuine democratic process in foreign policy will help secure peace. It was set forth by a British member of Parliament, Arthur Ponsonby, in 1915, following the outbreak of World War I, which Ponsonby considered a demonstration of the failure of the elite model of decision-making:

> When a small number of statesmen, conducting the intercourse of nations in secrecy, have to confess their inability to preserve good relations, it is not an

extravagant proposal to suggest that their isolated action should be supplemented and reinforced by the intelligent and well-informed assistance of the peoples themselves.[16]

These views about how much public democratic influence there ought to be in foreign policy are normative ones. What is the actual situation in the real world? There is no straightforward answer. Later in this section some empirical studies of the issue will be described, but first the argument concerning a possible incompatibility between democracy and the conduct of foreign policy will be analyzed. One author listed three points in support of the argument that democracy and foreign policy are incompatible.[17] The first concerns the conditions involved in bargaining with outsiders. Democratic openness and the internal disunity associated with democracy can lead to poor results in a process of bargaining. Furthermore, it seems wise to leave such negotiations in the hands of professionals, who are the experts in bargaining. There is also the need for secrecy, which is difficult to meet if foreign affairs are subjected to normal democratic debates and procedures.

The second point concerns the stakes involved in foreign policy. Foreign policy concerns the security of the nation, its survival. Therefore, citizens cannot afford, so runs the argument, to put such issues to open and free debates. It is critically important that they unite behind their leaders; opposition under such circumstances is not only disloyal, it may imperil the safety of the nation.

Finally, there is the issue of remoteness. Foreign affairs are far removed from the bread-and-butter issues that dominate domestic politics, with their clear implications for individual citizens. It is not that foreign policy is unimportant. It is simply that it is much more difficult for ordinary citizens to see the consequences that specific foreign policy options will have on their lives than it is for them to anticipate the outcome of domestic policies. It follows from this argument that foreign affairs should play an unobtrusive role in the political deliberations of the voters. The majority of voters feel that such matters can be left to the experts.[18]

An argument made against these three points is that they fail to differentiate between the various issue areas of foreign affairs. A common distinction is between the high politics of national security and the low politics of other foreign policy areas, such as those concerned with trade, finance, investment, the environment, and a host of other issues. It is clear that the points concerning the incompatibility between democracy and foreign policy pertain to the area of high politics rather than to the area of low politics.[19] But even in the area of national security, it can be said that from a democratic viewpoint it is simply unacceptable to leave issues isolated from the normal mechanisms of democracy. This normative debate will not be pursued further here. In what follows, I shall focus on some empirical investigations concerning the actual degree of democratic influence on the high-politics area of foreign affairs.

One problem facing such investigations is the difficulty in determining what is actually meant in operational terms by more democracy and less democracy in foreign affairs. In most cases, focus is on the role of public opinion. To what extent does public opinion influence the high-politics area of foreign policy? A recent study by Thomas Risse-Kappen compared the role of public opinion in the various responses of four countries—the United States, France, Germany, and Japan—to changes in Soviet foreign policy from Leonid Brezhnev (late 1970s) to Mikhail Gorbachev (late 1980s).[20] His conclusion was that mass public opinion does matter in each country; policymakers in liberal democracies do not decide against an overwhelming public consensus. However, the author went on to say that "there are discernible limits to the impact of the general public on foreign and security policies. Rarely does general public opinion directly affect policy decisions or the implementation of specific policies."[21] He argued that the major impact of the public is indirect, through its influence on elite groups. The elites have the final say, but elite groups whose opinions are in line with public preferences are likely to prevail. Finally, Risse-Kappen contended that variations in domestic structures in the four countries can explain the differences in policy outcomes that were sometimes seen even when there were similar public attitudes and similar influences from the international environment. Domestic structures encompass three elements: the degree of centralization of political institutions, the degree of state dominance over policy networks, and the degree of polarization between groups in society.

Other studies confirm the view that public opinion does matter in foreign affairs, albeit not in a direct manner but through the influence on elite groups. In the words of Bruce Russett and Harvey Starr, public opinion affects policy primarily

> *by setting broad limits* of constraint and identifying a range of policies within which decision makers must choose if they are not to face retaliation in competitive elections. These constraints are clearly quite broad, though they are likely to be felt more intensely the closer a particular decision time is to a national election. Of course, this still begs the question about how strongly mass opinion is itself merely shaped or controlled by elites who command public attention and the mass media.[22]

What light do these studies shed on the debate concerning the domestic aspect of democracy and peace? We started with the straightforward assertion by Kant that democracies will be peaceful because citizens will see to it that governments stay out of bloodshed and war. It seems that the link between the views of citizens and the outcomes in terms of foreign policy decisions is much more indirect, blurred, and complex than indicated by Kant. The restraint shown by democracies in their relations with other democracies is not directly attributable to the influence of peace-loving citizens on the decisionmakers.

Thus, it appears necessary to look for other factors that can help explain peace between democracies. One possibility that is consistent with Kant's general framework is that democracy promotes norms and expectations among citizens as well as among policymakers that support the peaceful resolution of conflicts with other democracies. Here, the decisive element is not the constraining influence of citizens on elites; it is the democratic political culture, which holds that "states have the right to be free from foreign intervention. Since morally autonomous citizens hold rights to liberty, the states that democratically represent them have the right to exercise political independence. Mutual respect for these rights then becomes the touchstone of international liberal theory."[23] This democratic political culture rules out ideological motives for democracies to act in expansionist ways against one another and makes it extremely difficult for democratic elites to legitimate wars against other democracies.[24]

Furthermore, democracy helps remove some of the important reasons for expansionism and the quest for domination that characterized regimes before the advent of democracy. External belligerence could flow from the desire of nondemocratic rulers to bolster their domestic positions; it could also stem from the rulers' quests for recognition, not only from their own subordinates but from other states as well.[25] In democracies, the recognition of leaders rests on a qualitatively different foundation. Democratic regimes may still go to war against states that they regard as illegitimate, but the democratic political culture makes it very difficult for them to wage war on regimes that are based on a democratic legitimacy.

The core of the matter is that democratic norms of peaceful conflict resolution and democratic norms recognizing other peoples' right to self-determination introduce an element of restraint or caution in the way in which democracies conduct international relations. These domestic elements of the democratic political culture help explain the peaceful relations between democracies. In a moment we will discuss the international dimension, but first it is useful to consider this domestic element in relation to the current processes of democratization.

*   *   *

We have made the argument that the peaceful behavior of democracies is predicated upon the existence of a democratic culture with well-defined norms concerning the peaceful resolution of conflict and the right of others to self-determination. If we wish to examine the prospects for a more peaceful world, a relevant question is therefore whether such a peaceful democratic culture can be found in the large number of democracies that are currently emerging.

In Chapter 2 it was demonstrated that the transition from a nondemocratic to a democratic form of regime is a long and complex process involving several overlapping phases. Three such phases were identified: the preparatory phase, characterized by a political struggle leading to the breakdown of the nondemocratic regime; the decision phase, where clearcut elements of a democratic order are established; and, finally, the consolidation phase, where the new democracy is further developed and where democratic practices eventually become an established part of the political culture.

It appears from this description that the emergence of a democratic culture is a long-term process that occurs as part of the consolidation phase. During this phase, democracy begins to be seen as "the only game in town" and both political actors and the population come to view democratic practices as the right and natural order of things. It was argued in Chapter 2 that the new democracies cannot be seen as consolidated; on the contrary, they were described as restricted, frail, and unconsolidated.

It follows that the norms of a democratic culture for the peaceful resolution of conflict have not yet become characteristics of the new democracies. A closer look at some of the recent transitions confirms this view. In Latin America, the military continues to be a dominant player in several countries. In some of them, domestic conflict has resulted in a breakdown of authority accompanied by a high level of domestic violence. In others, the rule of law has not yet been applied to the military, which continues to circumvent the democratic process. In Africa, the corrupt practices of personal rule remain strong in spite of the democratic openings. In Eastern Europe, a civil society is only beginning to emerge, and the rule of law is challenged by the *nomenklatura*, who have retained a good deal of power. In short, a democratic culture is beginning to emerge in the new democracies, but it is highly disputable whether this culture has grown strong enough to constitute the domestic basis for peaceful relations between democracies.

It is difficult to come up with a very definite conclusion in this area because we do not know the precise extent to which a democratic culture has to be developed in order to provide the necessary basis for peaceful relations. Michael Doyle has indicated that a democratic culture (which he called "the pacifying effects of liberalism") has to be deeply ingrained before it can form the basis for peaceful relations. Bruce Russett has emphasized that "it is not clear what threshold of democratic norms and practices must be crossed to achieve peace."[26]

With the continuing high levels of domestic violence in several Latin American and African countries, there are good reasons to be pessimistic.

Perhaps the best one can say is that a substantial number of countries are moving in the right direction for the moment—that is, they are moving in the direction of a stronger democratic culture. But it will certainly take some time before democratic culture is deeply ingrained, and there are no guarantees against setbacks or reversals.

The poor and institutionally feeble states in sub-Saharan Africa have particularly experienced increasing violent domestic conflict as a result of democratic openings.[27] It is extremely difficult to graft democracy upon weak states lacking the proper institutions and without a level of trust and mutual acceptance among contending groups of the elite and of the population. Democratization means better possibilities for formulating demands and openly discussing conflicts; this situation can easily lead to sharper confrontations and conflicts that can potentially undermine frail democratic openings.

One such threat comes from secessionist movements, which are frequently based on ethnic groups and exist in most of the weak states in sub-Saharan Africa. When the liberalization of media and improved organization rights give more voice to these ethnic groups, the democratic openings can stumble into a partially self-made roadblock, because a basic precondition of democracy is being questioned. That precondition concerns national unity, which as noted in Chapter 2, means that "the vast majority of citizens in a democracy-to-be . . . have no doubt or mental reservations as to which political community they belong to." It is exactly this premise that is questioned by secessionist movements. They want their own, independent political community. If that question is not resolved, democratization will most likely not proceed, and violent conflict will easily come back on the agenda.

Sadly, the two possible solutions to that question—namely, secession and changing the minds of ethnic and other secessionist groups about which political community they want to belong to—are both difficult to translate into practice. It is true that ethnic identities are malleable, but in many cases elite groups play on ethnic identities in ways that create more, not less, fragmentation and conflict. At the same time, the creation of a vast number of mini- or microstates is hardly a viable solution.

There may be other sources of conflict behind what appear as ethnic or nationalist demands. In weak states, political power is also economic power—the control of patron-client relationships based on the state apparatus. Control of the state means access to its resources in the form of jobs, contracts, opportunities for illegal gain via import permits, business licenses, and so on. The elite have little incentive to create an independent market economy, and politically, democratization means a less secure control of the state apparatus and its clientelist networks. Therefore, "for the political elites of a state that is collapsing economically as well as politically, nationalism has greater rewards—it can create new, protected ponds for the fish in danger of being eaten in the larger one."[28]

There are several instances in which early democratic openings have led to increased violent conflict and, in the most serious cases, to state collapse. In Sudan, democratization gave strong political voice to the Muslim organizations of the north, leading to a sharpened conflict with the non-Muslim south; that situation led to state collapse, with warlords fighting each other for control of territory. In Angola, the 1993 elections provoked more violent conflict; in Ethiopia, the Tigrean People's Liberation Front (TPLF), the dominant coalition party that took over after the fall of the Mengistu regime in 1991, attempted to avoid fragmentation by holding ethnic parties out of the election. The effort did little to promote democracy, and at the same time, it provoked a violent response from some of the ethnic groups.

In sum, stable, consolidated liberal democracy is the basis for the pacific union envisioned by Kant. But early processes of democratization and consolidated democracy are not the same. In weak states, early democratization often leads to more, not less, violent conflict. As a consequence, the process of democratization comes to a standstill or is rolled backward, and the pacific union remains a distant goal.

These considerations concern only the domestic basis for the pacific union envisaged by Kant. The possible zone of peace between democracies also contains an international dimension, which is the theme of the following section.

INTERNATIONAL RELATIONS: COOPERATION BETWEEN DEMOCRACIES

The international dimension of Kant's vision of peace between democracies is dependent on two related elements, one moral, the other economic. I shall treat them separately in the sections that follow.

Moral Aspects of Cooperation Among Democracies

According to Kant, the moral element that helps form the framework for peaceful relations between democratic states is based on the common principles of cooperation, mutual respect, and understanding. Such principles were indeed emerging in Europe in the early nineteenth century. It was a period during which the major European powers were expanding their territories in an attempt to achieve worldwide dominance, but it was also a time during which they worked out rules of behavior among themselves that can be seen as an important step toward the common standards envisaged by Kant.

The mutual understanding between the European powers rested on two basic principles: the recognition of the absolute sovereignty of states and the treatment of states as juridically equal.[29] On this basis, four principles came to form the framework for relations between the European states. The first was the balance of power, which has been called a systematic practice of anti-hegemonialism. The basic idea was that any state could be prevented from growing too powerful relative to the others through the shifting of alliances away from it, thereby hindering its rise to dominance. The second was the codification of a set of practices of interaction among states in order to form a body of international law. The third was the use of congresses for the purpose of settling the affairs of the European states; at the congresses, the states passed treaties to conclude wars and made additional agreements on general rules. The most important congresses were in Westphalia in 1648, in Utrecht in 1713, and in Vienna in 1815. The fourth was diplomatic dialogue. The application of the first three principles—balance of power, international law, and congresses—took place through diplomatic dialogue. Taken together the four principles formed the basis of a consensus among the European states. As one observer stated, "In the eighteenth century Europe came to be regarded as a single diplomatic commonwealth made up of a number of independent states 'resembling each other in their manners, religion and degree of social improvement,' or in other words operating within the framework of a common culture."[30]

It is important to emphasize that the European states did not form the full-fledged pacific union envisaged by Kant. The participating states were by no means full democracies, and the agreed-upon standards of behavior did not entirely rule out war between them. But Kant saw the pacific union as a long-term project, and many scholars view the standards of cooperation and common culture among the European states as an important first step. In recent scholarship, these relations between the European states have been looked upon as the foundation for an **international society.** Hedley Bull and Adam Watson defined an international society as

> a group of states (or more generally, a group of independent political communities) which not merely form a system, in the sense that the behavior of each is a necessary factor in the calculations of the others, but also have established by dialogue and consent common rules and institutions for the conduct of their relations, and recognize their common interest in maintaining these arrangements.[31]

If the relations between European states in the eighteenth and nineteenth centuries form the beginning of an international society, what is the present status of the international society? There is no uniform agreement about the common understanding that currently exists between the states in the world. A recent analysis by Barry Buzan argues that the present international society is in fairly good shape by historical standards. A main reason for its status is the fact that the sovereign territorial state is nearly universally accepted as the fundamental unit of political legitimacy: "The fundamental organizing principle of sovereign states treating each other as juridical equals reigns almost unchallenged as the basic political norm of the system."[32] On this basis, diplomacy and international law continue to provide a framework for cooperative behavior.

Kant regarded free communication as an important means of establishing a common international understanding, but he could hardly have foreseen the extent to which television and other mass media have, in the words of one observer, "brought the entire world to the instant attention of any listener."[33] The possibilities for instantly relaying information about events that occur anywhere in the world have dramatically improved the conditions for mutual insight and understanding among peoples and leaders alike. Some scholars speculate that a new global culture is emerging on the basis of these and related developments.[34] It is much easier to agree with their forecasts now than only a few years ago. The collapse of the totalitarian regimes and planned economies in Eastern Europe seems to have paved the way for a much stronger adherence to the norms of liberal capitalism—that is, to the combination of political democracy and a market economy. As was stressed in Chapter 1, systems based on these principles are not alike; they can take many different forms. But there appears to be a much higher consensus now regarding the adoption of the core features of liberal capitalism and the rejection of the two radical alternatives: fascism, on the one hand, and totalitarian communism, on the other.[35]

How do these developments relate to the prospects for peaceful relations among democracies that are bound by a common understanding? Following Kant's logic, we would expect that the general trends described here would be especially strong in the relationships between democracies with a common moral foundation. Consequently, we should expect norms to have developed between the democracies (especially the consolidated ones) that secure their devotion to the peaceful resolution of conflict.

This seems to be the case when we look at the relations among the well-established democracies in the industrialized West (including Japan). Western Europe, North America, Japan, Australia, and New Zealand have developed into a security community, which means that they constitute a group of states that do not prepare for, expect, or fear the use of military force in their relations with one another.[36] Several other factors have been important in the development of this security community, including economic cooperation and interdependence (on which I shall have more to say in a moment) and the cooperation between the Western powers in the alliance against the Eastern bloc. Yet, according to Kant's reasoning, the decisive element in the development of a security community between the partners in the Western alliance would not be the negative characteristic of a common enemy, but the positive shared foundation of democracy and cooperation. This view helps explain why violent hostilities could break out between the NATO partners Turkey and Greece in a period during which they were both governed by military dictatorships.[37]

However, the peaceful relations between the Western industrialized democracies have not been extended in equal measure to the democracies in the developing world. Relations between the United States and some democracies in Latin America provide an illustration. On a rhetorical level, the U.S. posture has been in perfect harmony with Kant's view of democracies seeking to promote democratic values in relations with other countries ever since Woodrow Wilson set forth the rules for his administration's relationship with Latin America:

> We hold, as I am sure all thoughtful leaders of republican government everywhere hold, that just government rests always upon the consent of the governed, and that there can be no freedom without order based upon law and upon the public conscience and approval. We shall look to make these principles the basis of mutual intercourse, respect and helpfulness between our sister republics and ourselves.[38]

In more recent times as well, the promotion of democratic values has been formulated as a guiding principle for U.S. policies. Yet both now and in the past, other elements of perceived national interest have competed with the goal of promoting democracy. Since 1945, an important issue has been the struggle against communism and Soviet influence in Latin America; another concern has been the protection of U.S. economic interests in the region. Both of these issues have been allowed to override concerns for the promotion of democracy on several occasions. A situation that occurred in the Dominican Republic in the early 1960s provides an instructive example. At that time a democratically elected leadership under Juán Bosch set out to promote economic development through nationalist economic policies that went against some American economic interests in the country. When Bosch faced the prospect of a military coup, Washington decided to opt for the authoritarian military dictatorship. John F. Kennedy formulated the alternatives as follows: "There are three possibilities, in descending order of preference, a decent democratic regime, a continuation of the Trujillo regime [a military dictatorship], or a Castro regime. We ought to aim at the first, but we can't really renounce the second until we are sure we can avoid the third."[39] Thus, fearing that the democratic Bosch regime would develop into a Castro regime, the

United States found it safest to back a military dictatorship. This action aided the struggle against communism and protected U.S. economic interests, but it hardly promoted democracy or economic welfare policies in the Dominican Republic.

A situation in Chile provides another example. In 1970, Chile already had a record as one of the most stable and long-lasting democracies in Latin America. The elections in 1970 brought Salvador Allende, a candidate backed by a left-wing Popular Unity coalition, to power. His economic policies aimed at redistributive reforms went against vested elite interests, including U.S. economic interests in Chile. Washington had attempted to prevent Allende's election through the support of rival candidates; after his election the United States became actively involved in supporting the opposition in the political parties, the Chilean military, and elsewhere.[40] The confrontation culminated in the military coup led by Augusto Pinochet in 1973, which paved the way for more than fifteen years of harsh military dictatorship in Chile.

It is not that the United States went to war with Allende's Chile; in that sense, Kant has not been disproved. Yet, as the events in Central America in the 1980s show, covert involvement with economic, military, and expert support for opposition forces can develop to a point where the distinction between such activities and open war becomes fairly academic.[41]

In any case, these and other examples are hardly evidence of Kant's expectation about democracies developing peaceful relations based on a common understanding and a shared moral foundation. Why do we see these hostile developments in relations between democracies? The reason for the hostilities in the examples given in this section are straightforward: The United States turns against some democracies because it fears that they will hurt U.S. economic interests or they will develop into communist regimes, which threaten U.S. security, or they will do both. Thus, not every kind of democracy is smoothly integrated in the pacific union envisaged by Kant; and it appears that those that are met with enmity instead of amity are the mass-dominated democracies, defined in Chapter 2 as regimes in which mass actors have gained the upper hand and push for reforms from below, attacking the power and privilege of the elites.

This situation creates two related dilemmas, one concerning the prospects for economic development and welfare improvement and the other the prospects for the peace between democracies. If international support (that is, support from the dominant countries in the developed world) is forthcoming only to the elite-dominated democracies, the possibilities for welfare improvement for the poor as a result of the democratic transitions may be very limited, as was argued in some detail in Chapter 3. And the resulting lack of welfare progress may threaten the prospects for the pacific union. As one scholar has argued, "Increasing worldwide adherence to democratic political norms and practices cannot alone bear all the weight of sustaining peace. Greater prosperity and economic justice, especially in the third world, must also bear a major part."[42] In short, the problem is that the necessary welfare progress may not be forthcoming when support is given only to the elite-dominated democracies, and the lack of welfare progress that results threatens not only economic improvement but also the possibilities for a pacific union.

How will relations between the dominant democracies in the North and the democracies in the South develop after the end of the cold war? It is too early to give a firm answer. On the one hand, there is basis for optimism: Because Soviet communism is no longer a threat, the dominant liberal democracies led by the United States ought to be able to accept the mass-dominated democracies in the South with more ease than before. The latter can no longer be seen as prospective allies of a world communist movement because such a movement no longer exists. On the other hand, post–cold war developments also give reasons for concern. The dominant liberal democracies, as well as the international organizations they lead, such as the International Monetary Fund and the World Bank, have made their provision of aid dependent on the new democracies' promotion of strictly liberal principles, such as privatizations, public sector cutbacks, free market policies, and the protection of private property.[43] During the 1990s, however, a more balanced approach appears to be gaining ground: Economic liberalization is set in a context that also involves social measures directed at the large groups of poor.

What about the new democracies in Eastern Europe? Even though the preferences of the leading Western democracies are for clearly liberal democratic systems in Eastern Europe, the scenario of Western support for an "East European Trujillo" is not likely. The countries in Eastern Europe share a common past with Western Europe and are in the process of reviving old relationships and building new ones. Several East European countries have joined the Council of Europe, whose very foundation is the recognition of common moral values of personal freedom, political independence, democracy, and the rule of law. Through the context of the Conference on Security and Cooperation in Europe (CSCE), all the East European countries including Russia have expressed their commitment to basic democratic values and the peaceful resolution of conflict. If the process of democratization proceeds successfully, there is reason to believe that most of the East European countries can become full members of the security community that has developed in Western Europe. Leading politicians in Poland, Hungary, and the Czech Republic have already expressed the wish that their countries become full members of the North Atlantic Treaty Organization (NATO). In the words of Czech foreign minister Jirí Dienstbier: "The only thing wrong with NATO is that we don't belong to it." The future may well see the North Atlantic Treaty Organization transformed into a Democratic Europe Treaty Organization.[44]

At present, the major problem in Eastern Europe is Russia. A continued process of successful democratization in Russia ought to facilitate its full incorporation into the community of liberal democracies. Yet some fear that NATO's expansion into Eastern Europe may antagonize Russia to such an extent that the democratization process in this country will be endangered. At the same time, the legitimate desires of several Eastern European countries to become NATO members must also be considered.

In the best possible scenario, further democratization in Russia and the expansion of ties with the West will resolve the problem. In the worst case scenario, democratization in Russia will suffer setbacks in part due to NATO expansion in Eastern Europe, and the threat of a new cold war will develop. Western democracies in NATO are attempting to solve this problem by combining NATO's expansion into Eastern Europe with additional security guarantees to Russia intended to allay any Russian fears of a new confrontation. Perhaps this is the best way to proceed, but the situation is difficult—not least because liberal democracy in Russia remains insufficiently consolidated.

In this section we have discussed Kant's vision of peaceful cooperation between democracies based on their common moral foundation. It was argued that such cooperation has indeed developed among the consolidated democracies of the North. In regard to relations with democracies in the Third World, the picture is less clear. Mass-dominated democracies there are seen as a threat to U.S. economic and security interests. They are met with enmity rather than amity. In Eastern Europe, several countries have good prospects for joining a larger European security community, but the relationship between such a community and Russia is much less certain.

Economic Cooperation Between Democracies

The final element upon which Kant's pacific union among democracies rests is economic cooperation. When countries focus on the spirit of commerce, they develop mutually beneficial ties of trade and investment as well as other economic relations. These ties, in turn, strengthen the bonds of peace among them.

The flow of goods and money, as well as of people, messages, and other forms of intercourse between countries, has indeed increased by leaps and bounds since the time of Kant's writing. As early as 1975, one scholar argued that "recent decades reveal a general tendency for many forms of human interconnectedness across national boundaries to be doubling every ten years."[45] Since the early 1980s, world trade has consistently grown much faster than world economic output. International financial flows have grown even faster than trade; for example, the London Eurodollar market, which borrows and lends dollars outside of the United States, turns over $300 billion each working day, which comes to $75 trillion a year.[46]

According to Kant's reasoning, economic exchange should be especially well developed among democracies. This premise also appears to hold true when we look at the Western industrialized democracies, but it is clear that other factors, such as the size of the national economy, the level of economic development, and the nature of economic policies, may play an even larger role than the presence of democracy in determining levels of economic intercourse.[47] Thus, a country with a large national economy, like the United States or India, has a relatively smaller share of its total economic activity crossing its borders than countries with small economies, like Costa Rica and Denmark. Countries with high levels of economic development, like Japan and Sweden, have much greater external trade than countries with low levels of development, such as Nepal and Bangladesh. Finally, countries with development policies aimed at the international market, for example, Taiwan and the Netherlands, have greater levels of external activity than countries with more inward strategies, such as China and North Korea.

In any case, there is a high degree of mutual economic dependence, or economic interdependence, among the Western industrialized democracies in Europe, North America, Japan, Australia, and New Zealand. These countries not only meet the third of Kant's conditions for a pacific union, economic cooperation, but also the other two discussed earlier, namely a developed democratic culture with norms of peaceful conflict resolution and a common moral understanding cultivated on this basis. They constitute a **security community,** which can be described as a contemporary version of Kant's pacific union. Karl Deutsch defined a security community as follows:

> A *security community* is a group of people which has become 'integrated'. By *integration* we mean the attainment, within a territory, of a *'sense of community'* and of institutions and practices strong enough and widespread enough to assure . . . dependable expectations of 'peaceful change' among its population. By sense of community we mean a belief . . . that common social problems must and can be resolved by processes of 'peaceful change'.[48]

In other words, although there may be problems within security communities that require change, and there may also be economic and other areas of conflict between the members, the groups within the security communities are determined to promote change and solve conflicts through peaceful means, without using threats of force.

It is more difficult to gauge the prospects for economic cooperation in Eastern Europe. On the one hand, as argued in Chapter 2, there is reason to be pessimistic concerning the possibilities for rapid economic transformation and world market integration of Eastern Europe. On the other hand, economic aid from the West to facilitate the economic changes appears to be forthcoming, and leading decisionmakers in the European Union foresee the admission of at least some East European countries to that organization by the end of the 1990s. The countries that are going to be admitted first are also those with the highest level of economic development: the Czech Republic, Poland, and Hungary. Their membership will help them develop ties of economic cooperation, which will strengthen their position in a European security community. In contrast, the less developed East European countries with looser ties to the Community will have more of a dependent "South status" in the realm of economic relations.

Let me now focus on North-South relations. There have not been many stable democracies in the South, and even the relatively few countries that are stable democracies have not experienced mutually rewarding economic relationships with the democracies in the North. North-South relations are characterized by unilateral dependence of the South on the North, not by mutually beneficial interdependence. Heeding the liberal advice of integrating in the international division of labor has produced mixed results in the South. The countries' dependence on exports of raw materials and agricultural products combined with the dominant presence of transnational corporations from the North in their domestic markets has not convinced the South about the mutually beneficial effects of economic exchange. In fact, some of the most successful countries of the South—including South Korea and Taiwan, the two most successful newly industrializing countries (NICs)—have used rather unliberal strategies of protection from the world market and have promoted a high degree of state intervention in the economy in order to get their economic development processes under way.[49]

For many years, radical theorists of development advised countries in the South to opt out of the international division of labor and look instead to economic self-reliance combined with cooperation among the poor countries themselves.[50] Today, most theorists advise the countries to find an optimal combination of integration in the world market and self-reliance. Unfortunately, they make these recommendations at a time when the problem of foreign debt is more serious than ever for many countries and the export market for typical southern products, such as raw materials and agricultural products, is stagnant or shrinking.[51]

Furthermore, the countries of the South are not equal members of the Bretton Woods system, the organizational system created at the end of

World War II to coordinate economic cooperation and development; and the two most important organizations from the South's point of view, the IMF and the World Bank, are dominated by the leading democracies of the North. As one scholar has said, "Although power is unequally distributed in the West, all members have access to both formal and informal management systems. In North-South relations, in contrast, there is no well-developed system with access for all. The South has been regularly excluded from the formal and informal processes of system management. North-South relations are controlled by the North as a subsidiary of the Western system."[52]

There seems no reason to expect substantial improvement in the position of the South in the international economic system as a consequence of the end of the cold war. If anything, there is reason to suspect change for the worse. With the end of ideological confrontation between East and West, the leading powers will be less interested in economically supporting friends in the developing world; the major Western donors will tend to focus on aid toward economic reconstruction in the East instead of in the South. To make matters worse, several of the South's export products will be met by increasing competition from the East in areas where the international market is stagnant.

Scholars often emphasize the need to differentiate between the various groups of countries in the South; and it is true that there are dramatic differences between the poorest countries in Africa at one extreme and the NICs in Southeast Asia at the other extreme. But none of these groups appears to be able to look forward to economic improvements in coming years. The NICs are being met with rising protectionism in their main market, the United States; they also have to face such internal problems as environmental degradation and demands for welfare improvement.[53] The poorest countries in Africa face a crisis of mere survival; many of them have been subjected to economic administration by the IMF and the World Bank, but the problems these countries face are so severe that the policies prescribed by the international institutions offer little hope for improvement in the short or medium run. Indeed, the World Bank itself admitted in a recent report that "the outlook for Africa is potentially devastating."[54]

Focus in this section has been on Kant's third basic pillar of a pacific union, mutually beneficial economic cooperation between democracies. Such economic cooperation has indeed developed between the stable, industrialized democracies in the West—that is, Western Europe, North America, Japan, Australia, and New Zealand. For the South, however, economic relations are characterized by dependence rather than interdependence. Integration in the world market has been a mixed blessing for the countries there; even with the end of the cold war, there is no prospect for an improved economic position for the South in the global system. Therefore, democracies in the South have not developed the mutually beneficial ties of economic cooperation with the leading democracies in the North that in Kant's view constitute the third necessary element of a pacific union. Prospects for Eastern Europe are better, especially for the countries that will join the European Union.

PEACE AS A RESULT OF DEMOCRACY?

In the past, democracies have not gone to war against one another, and the number of democracies in the world has increased rapidly in recent years. So will the spread of democracy bring a bright future with peace among nations? The theoretical foundation for expecting peace to flow from democracy is set forth by Immanuel Kant. His pacific union of democracies rests on three pillars: first, the mere existence of democracies with their culture of peaceful conflict resolution; second, the moral bonds that are forged between the democracies on the basis of their common moral foundations; and third, the democracies' economic cooperation toward mutual advantage.

This chapter has analyzed each of these conditions in the light of recent processes of democratization. With regard to the first, it is evident that a democratic culture with norms of peaceful conflict resolution has not yet developed in the new democracies. Democratic norms must be ingrained before the domestic basis of the pacific union will be secure, and such development of the political culture will take some time. There may be setbacks toward nondemocratic forms of rule.

The second condition is existence of common moral bonds between democracies. Such relations have indeed developed among the consolidated democracies of the West. Furthermore, there is reason to believe that the security community made up of the Western stable democracies can be extended to include the new democracies in Eastern Europe, provided there are no severe setbacks in their further democratization. The democracies in the South may or may not be included; in the past, the United States has turned against the mass-dominated democracies in the South in order to protect its perceived economic or security interests. If such policies continue, the pacific union is in double jeopardy: Mass-dominated democracies are left out and elite-dominated democracies in the South may well fail to produce the welfare progress that is necessary for a sustained peace.

The final condition is the existence of ties of mutually beneficial economic cooperation between democracies. Such economic interdependence is highly developed among the consolidated democracies in the West. At least some of the new democracies in Eastern Europe are set to be integrated into these economic networks through their anticipated membership in the European Union. For the democracies in the South, however, continued one-sided economic dependence rather than interdependence is the order of the day, even after the end of the cold war.

In short, the emergence of a global pacific union embracing all the new and old democracies cannot be taken for granted. The pacific union with its zone of peace is a long-term project. For the project to be successful, the three basic conditions laid down by Kant must be met by all of the democracies. Presently, a pacific union is a reality among the industrialized democracies in the West, and it may expand to include several of the new democracies in the East. Yet most of the democracies in the South fail to meet at least two of Kant's conditions. And instead of exhibiting further progress, they may backslide toward authoritarian rule.

What are the consequences of the existence and expansion of a pacific union for the dominant theoretical paradigm in international relations—realism? The next section of this chapter addresses the realist critique of Kantian visions.

PEACEFUL DEMOCRACIES AND REALIST THOUGHT

Kant's vision of a peaceful world of democracies belongs to a school of thought labeled **idealism.** The basic notion of idealist thinking is the view that conflict and violence can be overcome if the world is organized according to certain principles. Harmony is possible if man gives priority to the "right" ideas; with regard to Kant, the right idea would be that of democracy. This notion is rejected by *realist* thought, which claims to analyze the world as it really is, not as it ought to be. In the real world, conflict is imminent due to forces inherent in human nature and due to the fact that the world's populations have chosen to organize in the form of independent, sovereign states that respect no authority outside or above themselves. Early realist thought stressed the quest for power and dominance stemming from human nature as the basic reason for conflict; more recent contributions, often termed neorealist, emphasize the structure of the state system as the reason. The sovereign states respect no higher authority than themselves; there is no world government. In that sense, *anarchy* is the basic feature of the state system. With anarchy conflict is imminent. States cannot really trust one another, and one state's attempt to increase its safety by increasing its weaponry is unavoidably a threat to the security of other states. In short, as long as there are sovereign nation-states, there will be a state-system characterized by anarchy. As long as there is anarchy, there is a threat of violent conflict. In such a system, perpetual peace as envisaged by Kant is impossible.

It is not surprising, therefore, that according to many neorealists, "the theory of peace-loving democracies is unsound."[55] It is the aim in this section to discuss John Mearsheimer's neorealist critique of Kant's visions of democracy and peace. It will be argued that the distance between an analysis based on Kant, on the one hand, and neorealist thought, on the other, is much smaller than implied by Mearsheimer. On the basis of a more nuanced concept of anarchy than the one employed by Mearsheimer, we will see that the results described in the discussion of democracy and peace are perfectly compatible with neorealist analysis.

Mearsheimer started by attacking the logic of Kant's theory linking democracy and peace.[56] The first point, as has been discussed, concerns the assertion that democracies are more peaceful than authoritarian systems because the people in the former are more hesitant to go to war. Mearsheimer noted that democracies are as likely to fight wars as are other systems and that the public may be no less war-prone than authoritarian leaders are. His arguments do not contradict Kant; the general warproneness of democracies has already been noted, as has been the fact that the restraint shown by democracies in their relations with other democracies is not directly attributable to the influence of peace-loving citizens on the decisionmakers. The suggestion offered here was that a democratic culture of peaceful resolution of conflict introduces an element of restraint in the ways in which democracies conduct international relations. This element alone is not enough to explain the existence of a pacific union among democracies, but it is one of the three basic pillars of the pacific union.

The next point made by Mearsheimer criticizes the notion of a common moral foundation between democracies—that is, the second pillar of a pacific union. He claimed that moral bonds compete with other factors that are drawing toward conflict instead of peace, such as nationalism and religious fundamentalism. However, Kant did not deny the existence of these countervailing elements. His claim was, quite simply, that in relations between democracies with ingrained democratic cultures the competing factors will, most likely, *not* override the common moral foundation. Mearsheimer did not provide examples to support his argument, probably because there are none.

We have now reached the central point in Mearsheimer's attack on the logic of the theory. His argument is worth quoting in full:

> The possibility always exists that a democracy will revert to an authoritarian state. This threat of backsliding means that one democratic state can never be sure that another democratic state will not change its stripes and turn on it sometime in the future. Liberal democracies must therefore worry about relative power among themselves, which is tantamount to saying that each has an incentive to consider aggression against the other to forestall future trouble. Lamentably, it is not possible for even liberal democracies to transcend anarchy.[57]

Kant was well aware of the possibility of reversals toward authoritarian rule. That countries may backslide in that way does not invalidate the notion of a pacific union. The decisive point in Mearsheimer's argument is his inference that because there can be setbacks, anarchy remains the basic feature of the system regardless of the form of regime of the state. Anarchy prevails with all its dreadful but unavoidable consequences of imminent conflict and risk of war. Thus, the basic disagreement between idealists and neorealists concerns whether anarchy will prevail and whether it can be modified or even abolished in a pacific union of democracies.

Is it possible for liberal democracies to transcend anarchy? To answer this question, we need to take a closer look at the concept of anarchy. We know that anarchy is a rather abstract and imprecise characteristic of relations between sovereign states. If we categorize the states of the world in different subsystems, it is possible to give a more precise description of the relations between states in each subsystem. Such subsystems have been termed **security complexes,** that is, "groups of states whose primary security concerns link together."[58] Europe, the Gulf, and South Asia are examples. It then becomes possible to analyze the patterns and degrees of amity and enmity exhibited by the states within a specific group in more precise terms. It seems that the vast majority of neorealist analyses recognize the point that different security complexes can exhibit different degrees of anarchy.[59]

Can we further identify these different degrees of anarchy? A Danish scholar has suggested the following distinctions: At one extreme is what might be called raw anarchy; security is built on alliances and a balance of power achieved by deterrence. At the other extreme is the security community as defined by Deutsch; member countries are determined to solve conflicts by peaceful means, without fighting each other physically. In between are two middle stations, an immature and a mature security regime.[60] In the former, conflicts between states dominate, but amity is also possible. In the latter, states exhibit greater cooperation than they would if they were following only their short-term self-interests.[61] Such a continuum is shown in the accompanying illustration. Power politics dominates relations at the raw anarchy extreme; peaceful cooperation toward mutual gain dominates relations at the security community extreme.

Raw anarchy	Immature security regime	Mature security regime	Security community

The version of anarchy that Deutsch called a security community is exactly the pacific union envisaged by Kant. It is thus perfectly possible, even on the basis of neorealist reasoning, to conceive of a pacific union—a security community between consolidated democracies. Note that the general concept of anarchy still applies to the states in a security community: They are sovereign states that do not recognize an authority above or outside themselves. At the same time, it is clear that ties of cooperation and interdependence dominate relations between states in a security community. Mainstream neorealist analyses of deterrence and balance of power are thus more applicable to states in raw anarchy relationships than to states in communities in which cooperation dominates.

Mearsheimer would object that such security communities may not endure; there can be backslides toward more raw forms of anarchy. He is right; Kant also feared such developments. But security communities can also develop toward even further integration, as is currently happening, according to many observers, in the European Union. The Union has taken over political functions that were earlier the prerogative of the single member states; if the process of integration continues along the present path, the result will be a united Europe, a new state, a new unitary international actor. Anarchy between the old member states would be ruled out for good because they would have accepted a new, central authority above the old nation-states. Contrary to Mearsheimer's argument, it thus appears that it *is* possible for liberal democratic states to transcend anarchy. It must be emphasized, however, that the process of integration in the Union has not yet reached this point.

This takes us to the second path of criticism brought forward by Mearsheimer. He claimed that history provides no clear test of the theory that democracies do not fight each other. He raised the objection that several democracies have come close to fighting one another—for example, the United States and Allende's Chile. If Wilhelmine Germany is classified as a democracy, or a quasi-democracy, then World War I becomes a war among democracies. But these examples stem from the misunderstanding that the pacific union springs into existence between countries as soon as they meet a minimum definition of democracy. It does not. The pacific union is built upon a domestic foundation of democratic culture as well as two international pillars. All three must be in place for the pacific union to be effective, which is not the case in these examples.

Mearsheimer's other complaints concern the lack of a proper test of the theory of peaceful democracies. He pointed to the fact that democracies have been few in number over the past two centuries, and thus there have not been many situations in which two democracies have been in a position to fight each other. When there actually have been such situations, Mearsheimer's claim is that "there are other persuasive explanations for why war did not occur. . . . These competing explanations must be ruled out before the peace loving democracies theory can be accepted."[62]

If a proper test of the theory must meet Mearsheimer's requirement that all other competing explanations be ruled out, then there will never be a proper test of the theory. In international relations, as well as in other branches of social science, there is no possibility for laboratory experiments. One cannot in a clinical fashion isolate one single factor, such as democracy, from all other possibly relevant factors in the relationships between countries. The same constraints also pertain to Mearsheimer's theory of peaceful relations between states, which comes out of mainstream neorealism. He claimed that periods of peace between democracies (as well as between all other types of regimes) are due to patterns of alliances in the anarchic state system; in short, two or more states hold together because they face larger threats from other states in the system. Again, it is not possible to completely isolate this element of alliance patterns from all other possibly relevant factors. Theories in social science cannot be subjected to this kind of testing. It should be added that Mearsheimer would have a hard time explaining the hostilities in the 1970s between NATO countries Greece and Turkey with his theory of peace, which focuses solely on alliance and threat patterns.

Although laboratory tests of these theories are not possible, recent historical developments may provide a fairly strong test of Kant versus Mearsheimer. The case is the security community in Western Europe. According to Mearsheimer, the absence of war among Western democracies since 1945 is explained by the Soviet threat; with this threat gone, the Western partners no longer have an external enemy to hold them together. Mearsheimer's theory would predict that relations among them will tend to deteriorate toward raw anarchy, maybe even war. According to Kant, the pacific union among the Western democracies rests on the three pillars of a democratic culture, a common moral foundation, and economic interdependence. Those pillars are not affected by the presence or absence of a Soviet threat. Thus, Kant's theory would predict that the security community will remain intact and perhaps even expand due to the process of democratization in Eastern Europe.

Mearsheimer's arguments are set forth in his article in the journal *International Security*, cited earlier in this section. Several other scholars have recently argued in the vein of Kant that the security community will remain in place.[63] As I have already indicated, I find the arguments for a continued security community much more convincing than Mearsheimer's raw anarchy scenario. Indeed, the current process of further integration in the European Union is a movement toward even stronger cooperation. If the process continues in this direction, it could lead, possibly, to anarchy being transcended.

CONCLUSION

Kant's theory of a possible pacific union between democracies is basically sound. But it is a mistake to think that a pacific union automatically extends to include countries that are in the early stages of a long and tenuous process of democratization or countries that have not developed moral bonds and economic interdependence. The current processes of democratization increase the possibilities for a larger pacific union, but by no means do they guarantee its realization. In particular, the prospects are poor for the inclusion of the new democracies in the South in the pacific union.

Finally, it is possible to accept Kant's vision without rejecting the basic insights of neorealism. The distance between Kant's idealism and neorealism is often overdrawn, as in Mearsheimer's analysis. A pacific union is the type of anarchy called a security community. It is only when theorists place a one-sided emphasis on raw anarchy and see patterns of alliance and threat between anonymous states as the only factors leading to peace and war that there seems to be an insurmountable gulf between neorealist and Kantian thinking.

FIVE

□   □   □

The Future of Democracy
and Democratization

The preceding chapters have focused on the large number of transitions toward democracy in recent years and have examined the possible effects of these transitions on economic development and international relations. This chapter explores the future of democracy and democratization. Will the processes of democratization continue in force with many more countries becoming democratic and with the new democracies moving toward greater democratic consolidation, or will there be reversals toward authoritarianism? It will quickly become apparent that forecasting is difficult; the ability to explain past events does not, unfortunately, necessarily mean that one can make accurate predictions about the future. What individual actors and social movements will do is to some extent unpredictable. But with the knowledge we have about the general framework that sets the stage for the actors, we can outline some possibilities in the form of scenarios. Although we cannot know if these forecasts will prove true, they can help inform our thinking about the future.

In a recent, much debated essay, Francis Fukuyama predicted the end of history. With the collapse of communism, he argues, there is no longer a viable alternative to the Western type of liberal democracy that is based on a market economy. We are looking at, said Fukuyama, "the end of history as such: that is, the end point of mankind's ideological evolution and the universalization of Western liberal democracy as the final form of human government."[1] According to this reasoning, the liberal democracy model is more than merely dominant; it is the only one left to choose. The alternatives have proven unviable. The transitions toward democracy discussed in this book constitute the early stage of a process that will lead to the victory of democracy on a world scale.

Fukuyama's essay has attracted substantial critique. Samuel Huntington, a scholar who rejects Fukuyama's vision, is much more skeptical about the future of democracy:

History has proved both optimists and pessimists wrong about democracy. Future events will probably do the same. Formidable obstacles to the expansion of democracy exist in many societies. The third wave, the "global democratic revolutions" of the late twentieth century, will not last forever. It may be followed by a new surge of authoritarianism sustained enough to constitute a third reverse wave. That, however, would not preclude a fourth wave of democratization developing some time in the twenty-first century.[2]

Another line of argument against the "end of history" thesis is centered on the fact that democracy is not a fixed entity. Not only does it come in different organizational forms (parliamentary vs. presidential; majoritarian vs. representational; two-party vs. multiparty; and so forth), but there are also qualitative differences between the various concepts of democracy that have been put forth. Consider, for example, the two concepts outlined in Chapter 1: the narrow one by Joseph Schumpeter, where democracy is a method for choosing political leadership, and the comprehensive notion by David Held, where democracy is defined as a system in which individuals are free and equal in the determination of the conditions of their own lives. With Held's notion of democracy, the electorate has a greater influence on the state than Schumpeter allows. In addition, the people directly participate in local community institutions and manage cooperatively owned enterprises. This latter element highlights the fact that the two definitions also carry dissimilar implications for the political control of the economic sphere: from the rule of market forces based on private property, on the one hand, to a very high degree of political influence and control over the economy, on the other.

These models may be extremes, but they illustrate the significant diversity that continues to exist within the boundaries of democracy. In short, the necessity to navigate among these varieties of democracy is hardly compatible with the notion of end of history.[3]

This debate relates to the dilemmas of democracy and democratization discussed in this book. Democracy has made great progress throughout the world in recent years; but the characteristics of the new democracies call into question whether democratic advancement will continue and whether positive effects from democracy will be forthcoming. Chapter 2 stressed that the recent transitions from authoritarianism have resulted in frail, restricted democracies that are unconsolidated and plagued by severe social and economic problems. Chapter 3 emphasized that economic development and a general improvement of human rights are not necessarily forthcoming from these fragile democracies. Finally, Chapter 4 stressed that a more peaceful world will not necessarily be secured as a result of the present processes of democratization and that the inclusion of all of the new democracies in a pacific union is a long-term project with no guarantee of success.

It appears that future developments will take place on a playing field demarcated by two extremes. At one end is a very optimistic scenario in which democratic progress continues on all counts; more countries become democratic and the movement toward consolidated democracies takes place in the systems in which the democratic transition is already under way. At the other end is a pessimistic scenario in which a process of democratic decay sets in that may engulf not only the new democracies in the South and the East but also the consolidated democracies in the West. It is helpful to outline the two scenarios in more detail before proceeding to discuss what is likely to happen.

THE OPTIMISTIC SCENARIO: A SPRINGTIME OF DEMOCRACY

According to this scenario, the trend of democratization will continue in an increasing number of countries and will be accompanied by a democratization of the international system. One scholar has talked about the need, in a world of rapidly increasing interdependence, for **horizontal accountability,** which he defines as the representative mechanisms that "enable citizens to influence the decisions that are made in neighboring societies and that directly affect them."[4] In such a world, citizens of nation-states are profoundly affected by decisions made outside their borders, whether they concern political, economic, or environmental issues.

In the optimistic scenario, further democratization on national and local levels will lead to democratization on the level of the international system. The United Nations (UN) may be the point of departure. In earlier times, it was hardly possible to see the UN as an expression of a global popular, democratic will. It was an assembly of governments, many of which were authoritarian and unrepresentative. With further democratization at the national level, it will become possible to change the nature of the UN toward a genuine democratic world assembly. According to one scholar,

> Possibly, too, the United Nations can be weaned gradually away from the state system and begin to serve the cause of humanity as a whole, not naively, but rather fulfilling a mandate from a war-weary world to protect the planet from the adverse effects of antagonistic sovereign national wills and gradually incubating the growth and strengthening of world community structures and sentiments.[5]

Such developments can already be seen in some regional contexts, notably the European Union. Democratic organs above the states, on the Community level, are in the process of being strengthened in the context of further cooperation and integration.

Tendencies for democratization on the international level, according to this scenario, will go hand in hand with democratic deepening at the national level. In the consolidated democracies of the industrialized West, the peace dividend from the end of the cold war will be employed toward strengthening the welfare state and alleviating economic inequality. These developments will be combined with more democratic elements of participation and citizen's control in the local community and in enterprises, in accordance with the model of democratic autonomy outlined by David Held.[6]

In the East, democratization reinforced by advances in economic reform will dominate. The reintegration of the former planned economies into a network of European economic and political cooperation will significantly help the process. Hungary, Poland, and the Czech Republic will become members of the European Union at the turn of the twenty-first century; other countries will negotiate association agreements as a first step toward full membership. The more successful countries will set an example for the others. Thus, the "new" countries from the dissolved Soviet empire will emulate the democratic and economic reforms of their forerunners and will seek close collaboration with the European Union.

In the South, the time of the dictators will have finally ended. The great powers will no longer support nondemocratic regimes for national security reasons. Both the internal and the external pressures toward democratization will substantially increase. The rise of democracy will be supported by a process of demilitarization, which will reduce the influence of the armed forces in the developing societies. The regimes of long-standing dictators, such as Mobutu in Zaire and Daniel Arap Moi in Kenya, will finally begin to succumb to democratic forces. With the cold war over, a number of perennial conflicts in the developing world can finally be solved: in South Africa, Angola, Ethiopia, and Campuchea, for example. Perhaps even a peace settlement in the Middle East is conceivable. And it is not mere conflict resolution that will take place in these areas; the countries will be involved in the early steps toward democratization. With the existence of more democratic and responsive political systems, the road will be open to a process of economic development and increasing standards of living, which in turn will reinforce the process of democratization.

THE PESSIMISTIC SCENARIO: DEMOCRATIC DECAY

Globalization means the intensification of economic, social, political, and cultural relations across borders. Processes of globalization are increasingly important. But globalization may not lead to more democracy, as is implied in the optimistic scenario. Rather, the contrary is true of the pessimistic scenario. First, economic globalization is undertaken mainly by large transnational corporations (TNCs). In the 1980s, the six hundred largest TNCs accounted for close to one-fourth of the entire global production of goods. Today, the so-called free market trade between countries is not free at all; much of it is **intrafirm trade**—that is, trade across borders but between different units of the same corporation. In the early 1980s, close to one-third of the total exports from the United States, Japan, and the United Kingdom was in the form of intrafirm trade.[7] Second, globalization undercuts the ability of governments to regulate activities within their own borders. How can there be democracy in a meaningful sense if governments have little or no control over their economies and societies, because they are hooked into globalized markets and other global networks?

Third, from the viewpoint of the majority of the world's population, some of the most powerful organizations with a global reach are not very democratic. The **Group of Seven (G7)** is a case in point. This small group of the most economically (and militarily) powerful capitalist nations, made up of the United States, Japan, Germany, Great Britain, France, Italy, and Canada, calls the tune of the world economy with far-reaching implications for the majority of the world's peoples. It was to the G7, not to the economically powerless UN, that Mikhail Gorbachev turned for assistance for economic reform. For the poor countries of the South, the World Bank and the IMF are the more important organizations; but even if the scope of membership in these organizations is broader than in the G7, they are not democratic. They are controlled by a relatively small group of rich nations.

In short, it can be argued that the dominant international organizations are basically nondemocratic and that globalization means sharply deteriorating possibilities for a meaningful political democracy. This is the general background for democratic decay on the national level. Consider the consolidated democracies in the West, the heartland of victorious liberal democracy. Are we not forced to admit that there is no longer a vigorous political life in these countries? Instead, there is an increasing lack of interest in politics and a public debate characterized by diffidence and bereft of really significant issues. This argument was recently made in a number of French contributions to the debate on democracy.[8] The authors put some of the blame for democratic decay on a lack of political parties that are really different in important respects; only parties that are really different can raise debates about truly significant issues and sharpen our awareness of competing visions of the future. There is also a growing tendency for rising economic and social inequalities, which lead to political inequality. It is not that Western democracies will become authoritarian;

more likely the substance of democracy will simply dry up, and democracy in the West will become an increasingly empty shell of formal political practices made even more shallow by the negative impact of globalization.

In the East and South, democratic decay will be of a more tangible kind. The East will likely see a vicious circle of democratic decay reinforced by economic crisis. Aid from the West is far from sufficient to help secure a smooth passage toward a market economy. As the economic crisis grows, ethnic conflict will become more intense. A recent U.S. Times Mirror poll on European attitudes confirms the gloomy prospect for intensified ethnic conflict. The poll found that in every Eastern European country sampled, at least 40 percent of the respondents felt hostile to the main national minority.[9] Against a background of economic breakdown and ethnic confrontation, democratic consolidation cannot proceed. Old elites are called in by the disillusioned population to run proto-fascist governments that are turned against ethnic minorities.

The countries of the South will likely slide back and forth between restricted democracy and outright authoritarianism. Because the frozen, elite-dominated democracies are incapable of meeting popular expectations of economic improvement and further political reform, there will be an erosion of support for democratic institutions. The increasing social unrest will confirm the apprehension among elites that further democratization may indeed threaten their established dominance. At the same time, the decreasing support for democratic institutions will reduce the perceived costs of authoritarian solutions. Consequently, the military will again intervene in many countries, as it has already done in Sudan and Nigeria. The large majority of developing countries will again come under authoritarian rule.

WEIGHING THE ALTERNATIVES

When discussing possible future developments, we can probably be certain of only one thing: that reality will never come out as one-sided as depicted in the scenarios we painted, where the bleak future of across-the-board democratic decay stands against the hopeful vision of a total democratic victory. Reality will be something in between, a mixture of the two extremes. The hard part is predicting precisely what kind of mixture and what kind of flavor (optimistic or pessimistic) will dominate. To make such predictions would require a more concrete analysis of regions (South, East, and West) and specific countries within regions. In other words, we would need to take steps down the ladder of abstraction from the very general trends outlined in the scenarios toward more detailed analyses of specific areas. A complete analysis of this kind is not possible in the present context. Instead, let us look at the prospects for additional countries entering a process of transition toward democracy and the prospects for democratic advance in different parts of the world.

According to recent contributions by Robert Dahl and Samuel Huntington, we should not expect many more countries to become part of the present wave of democratization. Dahl emphasized that the conditions favoring democracy (polyarchy) are not strong in the presently nondemocratic countries; thus, we can infer that we should not expect a further spread of democracy.[10] Dahl also pointed out that in the consolidated democracies, countries that have been democratic for twenty years or more, the breakdown of democracy is extremely rare. Therefore, he concluded that

> neither the optimistic nor the pessimistic scenario is likely to prove correct. Short of a major catastrophe such as a deep and prolonged economic collapse or a nuclear war, polyarchy will continue in the large core of countries where democratic institutions have existed for a generation or more. At the margins of this core of stable democracies, transformations of both kinds are likely to occur.[11]

In other words, some countries may begin transitions toward democracy and others may backslide to authoritarianism; but the overall number of democracies will remain basically unchanged. Dahl made this conclusion before the recent changes in Eastern Europe, which bear witness to the fact that unforeseen events may occur. He did not predict the large number of transitions to democracy that were to occur in Eastern Europe. But the decisive push there was the lifting of Soviet dominance, and it is hard to think of other areas of the world in which actions by a major power could result in a similar drive toward democracy. Thus, Dahl's prediction may well apply to the global situation.

Huntington reached a conclusion that is similar to Dahl's. He noted that the large majority of the countries that democratized between 1974 and 1990 had some previous experience of democracy. The present ninety or more nondemocratic countries have always been nondemocratic. The fact that these countries have always been nondemocratic does not render democratization impossible, but it does make it more difficult.[12] Furthermore, many of the nondemocratic countries exhibit cultures, such as Islam or Confucianism, that are inimical to democracy. Like the situation just mentioned, such cultural traits do not render democratization impossible but make it more difficult. Finally, economic development and the eradication of poverty have been central features behind many of the earlier processes of democratization; but the prospects for rapid economic development in the poorest countries today are not good. Consequently, the lack of economic progress will inhibit a process of democratization. Huntington summarized as follows: "In China, the obstacles to democratization are political, economic, and cultural; in Africa they are overwhelmingly economic; and in the rapidly developing countries of East Asia and in many Islamic countries, they are primarily cultural."[13]

In sum, the prospects are not good for additional countries to join the most recent wave of democratization. What about the possibilities for further democratic consolidation in the new democracies? We may begin on an optimistic note: It is important to emphasize the rising global popularity of political democracy.

"Never in recorded history," wrote Robert Dahl in 1989, "have state leaders appealed so widely to democratic ideas to legitimate their rule," and the trend in this direction has grown even stronger since then.[14] Theorists who were earlier critical of democracy's potential now see it as the way forward; for example, a well-known Latin American scholar recently proclaimed that "democracy is the only path which Latin American countries can follow to modernity."[15] This statement is all the more remarkable when one notes that a widespread mistrust of political democracy had been prevalent in earlier periods among the popular forces in Latin America, which are now the central forces in the struggle for democracy. In Africa, the one-party system is no longer being supported as the ideal framework for consensual decision-making and for the promotion of economic and social development. Finally, in Eastern Europe, people no longer buy into the official position that political leadership by what was understood to be the party of the masses, the Communist party, is infinitely more democratic than liberal democracy on the basis of a capitalist society. On this point, the vast variety of new political movements in Eastern Europe are in agreement. As one observer noted,

> In politics they are all saying: There is no "socialist democracy," there is only democracy. And by democracy they mean multi-party, parliamentary democracy as practiced in contemporary Western, Northern, and Southern Europe. They are all saying: There is no "socialist legality," there is only legality. And by that they mean the rule of law, guaranteed by the constitutionally anchored independence of the judiciary.[16]

There appears to be only one major ideological opponent to the dominant idea of political democracy, and that is Islam. But even if Islam is strong in several countries in Asia and Africa, the current Islamic revival must be set against the quest for modernization that is also at work in the heartlands of Islam. In Saudi Arabia, the process of modernization has given democratic ideas a much stronger foothold.[17] At the same time, the case of Algeria demonstrates the paradoxical situation that democratic openings can bring forward Islamic forces at the elections, which were suppressed during earlier periods of authoritarian rule. Algeria will be an interesting case study of the extent to which democratic progress is at all compatible with a political scene distinguished by strong elements of Islamic forces.

In sum, the idea of democracy is robust at the global ideological level. Few authoritarian rulers would actively defend traditional, authoritarian modes of rule (North Korea and Iraq are possible examples). In the large majority of cases, authoritarianism is justified with reference to its supposedly positive ability to create order, stability, growth, and welfare. What was called the "Tocqueville factor" in Chapter 2, therefore, now works at a global level: Few dictators believe they have an inherent, legitimate right to be dictators. As one observer recently noted, "to live under autocracy, or even to *be* an autocrat, seems backward, uncivilized, distasteful, not quite *comme il faut*—in a word, 'uncool.' "[18]

This state of affairs provides some insurance against a comprehensive backslide to authoritarianism—but that certainly does not mean all is well, as we are painfully aware. What are the current prospects for democratic consolidation? This book has taken a somber view of those prospects. Chapter 2 concluded that most of the countries in transitions are not doing well as we approach the millennium; recent developments corroborate that judgment. One scholar, for example, has made a distinction between the shallow "electoral democracies" and the more democratically developed "liberal democracies." The best indicator of "liberal democracies" are those countries classified as "free" by Freedom House (see Chapter 1).[19] In contrast, "electoral democracies" may hold periodic elections and thus demonstrate some measure of political competition, participation, and liberties; parts of the population, however, may be held out of the political process, the military and other important sections of state power may be closed off from democratic control, the media may be censored, the courts may be corrupt and ineffective, and so forth. In short, elections take place, but democracy has not developed in most other respects. Examples of such "electoral democracies" are Brazil, Burkina Faso, Congo, El Salvador, Indonesia, Malaysia, Nepal, Russia, Turkey, and Ukraine.

While the number of "electoral democracies" has increased steadily, the number of more developed "liberal democracies" remains almost the same; there were seventy-six "liberal democracies" in 1991 and seventy-nine in 1996. Many countries remain shallow "electoral democracies," including some of the countries undergoing the most important recent transitions, such as Russia and Brazil. At the same time, the quality of democracy has deteriorated in a number of countries with long-term democratic experience: Venezuela, Colombia, India, and Sri Lanka.[20]

Prospects for Democratic Consolidation

Against this background, the immediate challenge is not so much one of imminent authoritarianism as it is of democratic consolidation—of pushing forward with the many institutional, economic, and social changes that will help develop and deepen democracy in the shallow "electoral democracies." The process of deepening democracies is one aspect of consolidation; the other aspect is the change whereby democracy becomes a more firmly embedded element of the political culture.

There is no theory that identifies the most important factors influencing the consolidation of democracy. A recent analysis argues that the level of economic development is a crucial factor in whether a country will sustain democracy: "Once a country is sufficiently wealthy, with per capita income of more than $6,000 a year, democracy is certain to survive, come hell or high water."[21] Yet the vast majority of recent transitions to democracy are below this economic level. What are the relevant factors for evaluating their chances for democratic consolidation? Several scholars have addressed that question.[22] They have come up with a number of different factors, some of which were introduced in the discussion of typical features of the current democratic transitions (Chapter 2). The most important factors are:

- the sequence of economic and political transformation;
- the legitimacy of political rule;
- institutionalized political parties;
- the strength of civil society.

The most severe problems in the sequence of economic and political transformation occur when economic liberalization and the consolidation of democracy must take place simultaneously. This is the case in Eastern Europe and in most of Latin America, including Brazil and Argentina. The problem is that the economic and political transformations are "governed by opposing social logics."[23] In the economic sphere, liberalization creates increasing social differentiation: There are winners and losers and only in the long run will substantially increased benefits exist for all. In the political sphere, there is increasing mobilization. The political mobilization of those groups negatively affected by economic reforms can create both political and economic problems and can lead to the "blocking or derailing [of] economic liberalization, the consolidation of democracy, or both."[24] In contrast, better conditions are likely for those countries that have undertaken economic reforms before democratization (e.g., Chile) or that have a longer democratic experience to draw on when they face the dislocations of economic reform (e.g., Venezuela).

The legitimacy of political rule is another important factor for democratic consolidation.[25] Consolidated democracies are based on a type of legitimacy that Max Weber called "rational-legal": The population accepts the authority of rulers, not because of their individual personalities, but because the system under which these rulers won and now hold office is accepted and supported. For this type of legitimacy to prevail, the source and the agent of legitimacy must be separated. This separation is especially difficult in systems in which the regime's legitimacy has rested on people's faith in a personal leader—what Weber called charismatic legitimacy. The personal rule systems in Africa, for example, are based on charismatic legitimacy, which makes democratic consolidation in these countries especially difficult, because the whole basis for legitimate rule has to be changed. The more such nonrational-legal forms of legitimacy are entrenched, the higher the difficulties for democratic consolidation become.

Political parties are crucially important for democratic consolidation. As mentioned in Chapter 2, democracy introduces an element of uncertainty into the political process. Democratic institutions, especially a stable party system, help to reduce uncertainty, because "actors know the rules and have some sense of how to pursue their interests. . . . Democracy has generally thrived when party systems have been institutionalized."[26] Institutionalization of political parties means that they emerge as valued and stable elements in the political process.[27] Many countries in Africa, Asia, and Latin America do not have institutionalized party systems; such a situation hinders the process of democratic consolidation for these countries. In contrast, countries possessing such a system (e.g., Uruguay and Chile) have much better prospects for democratic consolidation.

Political parties are part of the larger system of non-state institutions called civil society. An effective civil society—a dense network of associations, interest groups, civil rights groups, and so forth—is the best basis for the consolidation of democracy. In a number of new democracies, including those in Eastern Europe and Russia as well as in several countries in the South, an effective civil society is only in the process of being established; these countries thus face additional problems for democratic consolidation.

In sum, there are numerous unconsolidated, "electoral democracies" in the world with differing prospects for further consolidation. The four factors mentioned previously are among the most important determinants of those prospects. In countries where those factors are favorable, we should expect a high success rate for democratic consolidation, and vice versa. In several countries, all four factors mitigate against democratic consolidation; in others, the picture is mixed. Few if any countries present optimal prospects for democratic consolidation on all four counts—hence the current skepticism regarding prospects for democratic consolidation.

Democratic Decay in Established Democracies?

The previous considerations concern prospects for the new democracies; I have also examined the possibilities for additional countries to join the wave of democratization. One final item important to the future of democracy must be considered: the possibilities for continued democratic vitality in the established, industrialized democracies. In a highly debated contribution, Robert Putnam recently argued that there is currently a loss of "social capital" in the United States, which has negative implications for the quality of democracy. Social capital is defined as "features of social organization, such as trust, norms, and networks, that can improve the efficiency of society by facilitating coordinated actions."[28] The leading indicator of social capital is the rate of membership in voluntary associations, for example, in amateur soccer clubs, choral societies, hiking clubs, and literary circles. Such membership has dwindled in the United States. Bowling clubs, for example, experienced a 40 percent decrease in membership between 1980 and 1993, yet the number of bowlers during the same period increased by 10 percent. Putnam argues that such a decrease in social capital will undermine the vitality of democracy in many established, wealthy democracies.

Although critics see both theoretical and empirical problems with Putnam's analysis,[29] his contribution does emphasize the important point that democracy cannot be taken for granted; indeed, it is a process that requires continued input to remain vital and vigorous. One crucial element in maintaining a democracy, therefore, is the active participation and support of a large majority of the population. With the decline in social capital, the conditions for such popular participation and support are increasingly adverse.

The other great challenge to established democracies comes from globalization. As indicated earlier, globalization may undermine democracy because national governments have less and less control over what happens within their own borders. National leaders may be elected according to strict democratic principles, but what does that help if they are left almost powerless to manage national affairs because economic and other developments are decided by outside factors over which they have little control?

In approaching this question, we should keep in mind that the extent to which globalization challenges a country's democracy remains a highly debated issue. Some scholars argue that the negative effects of globalization are exaggerated—that there is still much scope for democratic governments to influence national development. In fact, globalization is sometimes used by politicians as an excuse to do nothing, to be passively reactive rather than actively regulating and managing national affairs.[30]

Other scholars emphasize that globalization profoundly affects conditions for national policy-making by limiting the maneuvering room of national governments.[31]

We cannot fully settle this debate here. Globalization undoubtedly affects different countries in different ways. In particular, we should expect large countries such as the United States to be much better able to control events than small countries such as Denmark. But recent analyses have also demonstrated that globalization does affect larger countries, especially in undermining "governments' authority in the domain of macroeconomic policy."[32]

How can democracy face the challenge of globalization? To resort to isolation—an attempt to shut off the country from outside influence—is hardly a way out. Globalization involves cooperation with others for mutual benefit; the industrialized democracies, for example, reap great welfare benefits from globalization. In an increasingly interdependent world, isolation does not benefit a nation's welfare, as demonstrated by North Korea and a few other countries.

One way to proceed is via regional integration, as in the case of the European Union. The EU cooperation can be understood as an attempt by member countries to reclaim some of the influence they lost at the national level due to forces of globalization. Intense cooperation means an opportunity to influence policies in other countries and thereby directly affect the external environment at the European level.

From a democratic point of view, however, EU cooperation has two problems. First, while in gaining influence over others, countries must in turn allow other countries increased influence over them. But how much can small countries decide in regional and international fora; are they not forced to follow the lead of the big and strong? Second, the EU's supranational structures of governance are in some ways less democratic than those of national parliaments and governments. Some have claimed that there is a "democratic deficit" in the EU, because many decisions are left to bureaucrats with no clear democratic mandates or to divisions such as the Commission, in which deliberations are not sufficiently open to democratic scrutiny. One solution is to proceed to a more genuine federal structure in EU cooperation, but member countries are not yet ready to go that far.

The case of the EU demonstrates the difficulties in constructing supranational levels of governance that live up to the demands of democracy we have learned to expect from our experiences at the national level. If such regional organizations have problems with democracy, we must expect even larger problems in attempts to construct truly global structures of governance. Some scholars have begun to contemplate a "cosmopolitan democracy with global reach,"[33] in which countries respond to the challenge of globalization by constructing a new democratic framework based not on the nation-state but on a democratic structure with global reach. David Held, for example, envisions a cosmopolitan democracy in which people have multiple citizenships: "They would be citizens of their immediate political communities, and of the wider regional and global networks which impacted upon their lives."[34]

The idea of multiple citizenship indicates the magnitude of the challenge to democracy contained in processes of globalization. Remember the precondition for democracy spelled out by Rustow in Chapter 2: People must have no doubt or mental reservation about which political community they belong to. Contrast this with the notion of multiple citizenship, in which people are citizens of local, national, regional, and supraregional communities. Cosmopolitan democracy is very different from the democracy in an independent country. And we have only begun to speculate about democracy in a global setting. Globalization, then, presents a profound challenge to democracy, especially in the developed, industrialized parts of the world—which are also the most touched by processes of globalization.

In short, the process of democratization must continually face and respond to new problems. A democracy can never be taken for granted, not even in those parts of the world where it appears to be the most firmly entrenched.

CONCLUSION

The discussion about the meaning of democracy in Chapter 1 formed the basis for our assessment of the processes of democratization under way in many countries and for our examination of the possible domestic and international consequences of democracy. A basic dilemma was identified at the beginning: The democratic openings we have seen are a mere beginning; by no means do they ensure further democratization or additional benefits in the form of economic development, peace, and cooperation. Each of the main chapters in this book has focused on a particular aspect of this dilemma: the processes of democratization in Chapter 2, the consequences for economic development and human rights in Chapter 3, and the consequences for peace among nations in Chapter 4. In Chapter 5, the future of democracy and democratization was evaluated against the framework of an optimistic and a pessimistic scenario. If our final assessment leans toward the pessimistic scenario, we may do well to remember a fundamental lesson learned in recent years: The future is not predetermined; expected patterns of development can be fundamentally changed by the actions of individuals and groups on both the local and the national level. It is the sum of these actions that determines whether democracy will prevail. Perhaps to a higher extent than ever before, the responsibility for future developments rests heavily with the actors in the democracies of the industrialized countries—that is, with us. Not only are we responsible for the way in which democracy fares in our own part of the world; we also control the basic framework of the international system, the economic, political, and ideological dimensions of which influence the possibilities of democratization in the South and the East. Our willingness to contribute to the solution of economic and other problems in these regions is of major importance for their future prospects for democratization. Furthermore, if the dilemmas of the current processes of democratization carry any weight, we are forced to be more concerned not only with democracy in general but also with the specific kinds of democracy that are emerging in the present world. Support for elite-dominated, restricted democracies will not be enough. Ways must be found to deepen and strengthen democratic processes. Today's fragile democracies are a step ahead of yesterday's authoritarian systems, but real, sustained progress will require further democratic consolidation.

□ □ □

Discussion Questions

Chapter One

1. Give a broad and a narrow definition of democracy. What are the arguments in favor of each?

2. According to Julius Nyerere, the former president of Tanzania, the struggle for freedom in the Third World is primarily a struggle for freedom from hunger, disease, and poverty, and not so much a struggle for political rights and liberties. Is that true?

3. In 1968, a progressive military junta took power in Peru and did away with the democratic political system. The military government went on to launch much more far-reaching measures against poverty and poor living conditions for the mass of people than had been seen under the previous, democratic government, which was dominated by an elite. Which regime is more democratic: the one that upholds a democratic political system that serves mainly an elite or the one that does away with the democratic political system in order to promote the struggle for freedom from hunger, disease, and poverty?

4. Discuss the assertion that only a capitalist system can provide the necessary basis for democracy. Which elements in capitalism can promote democracy and which can impede it?

Chapter Two

1. Some conditions favor the rise of democracy more than others. What are the most favorable economic, social, and cultural conditions for democracy? Why is it that democracy may emerge in places where the conditions for it are adverse?

2. Are there common factors that help explain the recent surge toward democracy in many countries, or must democratization in different parts of the world be explained in different ways?

3. Outline the phases in the transition toward democracy according to the model described in this chapter and apply the model to your own country. Is your country a consolidated democracy? How much time has passed since the move toward democracy began in your country? What light does the experience of your own country shed on the process of transition to democracy in other countries?

137

4. What arguments can you make for and against the assertion that democracy has made great progress in the world during the past decade?

Chapter Three

1. What arguments have been made in support of the view that there is a trade-off between political democracy and economic development? What arguments have been made against this view? Is it possible to settle this debate on the basis of empirical analyses?

2. This chapter identifies three types of authoritarian systems: authoritarian developmentalist regimes, authoritarian growth regimes, and authoritarian state elite enrichment regimes. Which of these types is the most common today? How do elite-dominated and mass-dominated democracies differ?

3. Sometimes the early process of democratization brings neither welfare improvement nor a better human rights situation. Is this an argument against democracy?

Chapter Four

1. What are the arguments in favor of the contention that the spread of democracy will lead to the creation of a peaceful world? Democracies have not gone to war with one another in the past, but they have been few in number and have not had many opportunities to fight one another. Is this knowledge about the past a reliable guide to the actions of democracies in a future world where, possibly, a large number of democracies can come into conflict?

2. Do you think that a more peaceful world will result from the current processes of democratization? Why or why not?

3. Evaluate current developments in the European Union in light of the debate between a Kantian view and Mearsheimerian neorealism. Which of these views, if either, is correct?

Chapter Five

1. What arguments can you give in support of the optimistic and the pessimistic scenarios that were described as a basis for discussion of the future of democracy and democratization? Is the trend in your own country toward more or less democracy? In what way?

2. What would a really democratic world order look like? Would it not be dominated by the poor majority of the world's population from China, India, and elsewhere in the South? And would the major policy aim of such an order not be the redistribution of wealth from North to South?

□ □ □

Notes

Chapter One

1. David Held, *Models of Democracy* (Cambridge: Polity Press, 1987), p. 2.

2. Ibid., pp. 28–33. See also Arne Naess et al., *Democracy, Ideology, and Objectivity* (Oslo: Oslo University Press, 1956), p. 78n.

3. Held, *Models of Democracy*, p. 32.

4. C. B. Macpherson, *The Life and Times of Liberal Democracy* (Oxford: Oxford University Press, 1977), p. 13.

5. Held, *Models of Democracy*, p. 41n.

6. See Goran Therborn, "The Rule of Capital and the Rise of Democracy," *New Left Review* 103 (1977): 3.

7. Macpherson, *The Life and Times*; see also Held, *Models of Democracy*.

8. See Macpherson, *The Life and Times*, pp. 35–39.

9. Held, *Models of Democracy*, p. 69.

10. F. A. Hayek, *The Constitution of Liberty* (London: Routledge and Kegan Paul, 1960), p. 103.

11. See Held, *Models of Democracy*, pp. 248–252.

12. Quoted from ibid., p. 248.

13. See ibid., p. 86.

14. See ibid., p. 94.

15. See Macpherson, *The Life and Times*, pp. 60–64, and Held, *Models of Democracy*, pp. 100–104.

16. Quoted from Held, *Models of Democracy*, p. 75.

17. Macpherson, *The Life and Times*; Carol Pateman, *Participation and Democratic Theory* (Cambridge: Cambridge University Press, 1970); Carol Pateman, *The Problem of Political Obligation: A Critique of Liberal Theory* (Cambridge: Polity Press, 1985).

18. Pateman, *Participation and Democratic Theory*, p. 110.

19. See the discussion of Marx in Held, *Models of Democracy*, pp. 105–143.

20. Robert A. Dahl, *A Preface to Economic Democracy* (Cambridge: Polity Press, 1985), p. 60.

21. See, for example, Carol C. Gould, *Rethinking Democracy* (New York: Cambridge University Press, 1988).

22. For a summary of the current debate, see Charles F. Andrain, "Capitalism and Democracy Revisited," *Western Political Quarterly 37*, no. 4 (1984): 652–664.

23. Joseph Schumpeter, *Capitalism, Socialism and Democracy* (1942; reprint, London: Allen and Unwin, 1976), p. 260.

24. Held, *Models of Democracy*, p. 271.

25. Ibid., p. 285.

26. Carl Cohen, *Democracy* (New York: Free Press, 1971), p. 109n; see also Gavin Kitching, *Rethinking Socialism: A Theory for a Better Practice* (London: Methuen, 1983), p. 49.

27. Francis Fukuyama, "The End of History?" *The National Interest*, no. 16 (1989): 3–18.

28. Robert A. Dahl, *Polyarchy: Participation and Opposition* (New Haven: Yale University Press, 1971), p. 3.

29. Hans-Jørgen Nielsen grouped these eight conditions in a similar way in *Den Chilenske Transitionsproces* (The Chilean process of transition) (Aarhus: University of Aarhus, Institute of Political Science, 1991), p. 5.

30. Larry Diamond, Juan J. Linz, and Seymour Martin Lipset (eds.), *Democracy in Developing Countries*. Vol. 2: *Africa* (Boulder: Lynne Rienner, 1988), p. xvi.

31. For such attempts at differentiation in African and Latin American countries, respectively, see Richard Sklar, "Democracy in Africa," *African Studies Review* 26, no. 3/4 (1983): 11–25, and Karen L. Remmer, "Exclusionary Democracy," *Studies in Comparative International Development* 20, no. 4 (1985–1986): 64–86.

32. Dahl, *Polyarchy*, p. 4.

33. Tatu Vanhanen, *The Process of Democratization: A Comparative Study of 147 States, 1980–88* (New York: Taylor and Francis, 1990).

34. See *Freedom Review* 28, no. 1 (1997). For a general survey of attempts to measure democracy, see *Studies in Comparative International Development* 25, no. 1 (1990).

35. *Freedom Review* 28, no. 1 (1997): 15.

36. Chalmers Johnson, "Political Institutions and Economic Performance: The Government-Business Relationship in Japan, South Korea, and Taiwan," in Frederic C. Deyo (ed.), *The Political Economy of the New Asian Industrialism* (Ithaca: Cornell University Press, 1987), p. 137. Emphasis added.

37. See, for example, Karl van Wolferen, *The Enigma of Japanese Power* (New York: Knopf, 1989).

38. See John Woronoff, *Politics the Japanese Way* (London: Macmillan, 1988); Roy Thomas, *Japan: The Blighted Blossom* (Vancouver: New Star, 1989).

39. Mark Gasiorowski, "The Political Regimes Project," *Studies in Comparative International Development* 25, no. 1 (1990): 112n.

40. *Human Development Report 1996* (New York: Oxford University Press, 1996). This report is published annually.

41. See Kitching, *Rethinking Socialism*, p. 48.

42. UNDP, *Human Development Report 1996*.

43. See Therborn, "The Rule of Capital."

44. See Robert O. Keohane and Joseph S. Nye, Jr., *Power and Interdependence: World Politics in Transition* (Boston: Little, Brown, 1977).

45. Robert A. Dahl, *Democracy and Its Critics* (New Haven: Yale University Press, 1989), p. 319.

46. Quoted from John Loxley, "The Devaluation Debate in Tanzania," in Bonnie K. Campbell and John Loxley (eds.), *Structural Adjustment in Africa* (London: Macmillan, 1989), p. 15.

47. J. R. Scott, *Comparative Political Corruption* (Englewood Cliffs, N.J.: Prentice-Hall, 1972), p. 137.

48. For an example of such a program, see O. M. Prakash and P. N. Rastogi, "Development of the Rural Poor: The Missing Factor," *IFDA Dossier* 51 (1986); see also Georg Sørensen, *Democracy, Dictatorship and Development: Economic Development in Selected Regimes of the Third World* (London: Macmillan, 1991), ch. 2.

49. See Mark Blecher, *China: Politics, Economics and Society* (London: Frances Pinter, 1986), p. 104.

50. Ibid., p. 25n.

51. Ibid., p. 26.

Chapter Two

1. Seymour Martin Lipset, "Some Social Requisites of Democracy: Economic Development and Political Legitimacy," *American Political Science Review* 53 (1959): 75. See also Seymour Martin Lipset, "The Social Requisites of Democracy Revisited," *American Sociological Science Review* 59 (1994): 1–22.

2. Samuel P. Huntington, "Will More Countries Become Democratic?" *Political Science Quarterly* 99, no. 2 (1984): 199.

3. Robert A. Dahl, *Polyarchy: Participation and Opposition* (New Haven: Yale University Press, 1971), p. 65.

4. Guillermo O'Donnell, *Modernization and Bureaucratic-Authoritarianism: Studies in South American Politics* (Berkeley: University of California, Institute of International Studies, 1973).

5. See Huntington, "Will More Countries Become Democratic?" p. 209.

6. See Terry Lynn Karl, "Dilemmas of Democratization in Latin America," *Comparative Politics* 23, no. 1 (1990): 4.

7. Barrington Moore, Jr., *Social Origins of Dictatorship and Democracy: Lord and Peasant in the Making of the Modern World* (Boston: Beacon Press, 1966), p. 418.

8. Goran Therborn, "The Rule of Capital and the Rise of Democracy," in David Held et al. (eds.), *States and Societies* (Oxford: Martin Robertson, 1983), p. 271.

9. See Huntington, "Will More Countries Become Democratic?" p. 206.

10. See, for example, Fernando Henrique Cardoso, "Dependent Capitalist Development in Latin America," *New Left Review* 80 (1973): 83–95.

11. Dahl, *Polyarchy*, pp. 202–208.

12. Larry Diamond, Juan J. Linz, and Seymour Martin Lipset (eds.), *Democracy in Developing Countries*. Vol. 2: *Africa* (Boulder: Lynne Rienner, 1988), pp. ix–xxix.

13. In Juan J. Linz and Alfred Stepan (eds.), *The Breakdown of Democratic Regimes: Crisis, Breakdown and Reequilibration* (Baltimore: Johns Hopkins University Press, 1978), p. 5. See also Dankwart A. Rustow, "Transitions to Democracy," *Comparative Politics* 2, no. 3 (1970): 337–365.

142 ☐ Notes

14. For a similar view, see Karl, "Dilemmas of Democratization."

15. Adam Przeworski, "Democracy as a Contingent Outcome of Conflicts," in Jon Elster and Rune Slagstad (eds.), *Constitutionalism and Democracy* (Cambridge: Cambridge University Press, 1988), pp. 59–81.

16. Ibid., p. 71.

17. See Guillermo O'Donnell and Philippe C. Schmitter, *Transitions from Authoritarian Rule: Tentative Conclusions About Uncertain Democracies* (Baltimore: Johns Hopkins University Press, 1986), p. 19.

18. Richard Sandbrook, "Liberal Democracy in Africa: A Socialist-Revisionist Perspective," *Canadian Journal of African Studies* 22, no. 2 (1988): 253.

19. See ibid., p. 254.

20. Przeworski, "Democracy as a Contingent Outcome," p. 69.

21. Ibid., p. 79.

22. This does not mean that changes have not occurred, only that changes toward more democracy in some countries have been accompanied by changes toward less democracy in other countries.

23. Huntington, "Will More Countries Become Democratic?" p. 197.

24. Donald Share, "Transitions to Democracy and Transition Through Transaction," *Comparative Political Studies* 19, no. 4 (1987): 545. See also three articles on which my remarks draw: Kenneth Medhurst, "Spain's Evolutionary Pathway from Dictatorship to Democracy," *West European Politics* 7, no. 2 (1984): 30–50; P. Nikiforos Diamandouros, "Transition to, and Consolidation of, Democratic Politics in Greece, 1974–83: A Tentative Assessment," *West European Politics* 7, no. 2 (1984): 50–72; Thomas C. Bruneau, "Continuity and Change in Portuguese Politics: Ten Years After the Revolution of 25 April 1974," *West European Politics* 7, no. 2 (1984): 72–83.

25. Francisco C. Weffort, quoted from Hélgio Trindade, "Presidential Elections and Political Transition in Latin America," *International Social Science Journal* 128 (1991): 301–314.

26. See Fernando Henrique Cardoso, "Democracy in Latin America," *Politics and Society* 15, no. 1 (1986–1987): 32.

27. Timothy Garton Ash, "Eastern Europe: The Year of Truth," *The New York Review of Books,* February 15, 1990, pp. 17–22.

28. Quoted from Ole Nørgaard, "De post-stalinistiske samfund og demokratiet" (The post-Stalinist societies and democracy), *Politica* 23, no. 3 (1991): 246.

29. Ash, "Eastern Europe," p. 19.

30. See Nørgaard, "De post-stalinistiske samfund," pp. 241–259.

31. See Adam Przeworski, "The 'East' Becomes the 'South'? The 'Autumn of the People' and the Future of Eastern Europe," *PS Political Science and Politics* 24, no. 1 (1991): 21.

32. See Samuel Decalo, "The Process, Prospects and Constraints of Democratization in Africa" (Paper delivered at the XVth World Congress of the International Political Science Association, Buenos Aires, July 21–25, 1991), p. 2.

33. Ibid., p. 8.

34. See Jacques-Mariel Nzouankeu, "The African Attitude to Democracy," *International Social Science Journal* 128 (1991): 374.

35. Quoted from Decalo, "Democratization in Africa," p. 11.

36. See Karl D. Jackson, "The Philippines: The Search for a Suitable Democratic Solution, 1946–86," in Larry Diamond, Juan J. Linz, and Seymour Martin Lipset (eds.), *Democracy in Developing Countries*. Vol. 3: *Asia* (Boulder: Lynne Rienner, 1989), pp. 231–267.

37. See Niranjan Koirala, "Nepal in 1990: End of an Era," *Asian Survey* 31, no. 2 (1991): 134–140.

38. Rustow, "Transitions to Democracy."

39. Ibid., p. 350.

40. W. Ivor Jennings, quoted from ibid., p. 351.

41. Rustow, "Transitions to Democracy," p. 354.

42. Alfred Stepan, "Paths Toward Redemocratization: Theoretical and Comparative Considerations," in Guillermo O'Donnell, Philippe C. Schmitter, and Laurence Whitehead (eds.), *Transitions from Authoritarian Rule: Comparative Perspectives* (Baltimore: Johns Hopkins University Press, 1988), pp. 64–85.

43. O'Donnell and Schmitter, *Transitions from Authoritarian Rule.*

44. See Nørgaard, "De post-stalinistiske samfund," p. 14.

45. Rustow, "Transitions to Democracy," p. 355.

46. O'Donnell and Schmitter, *Transitions from Authoritarian Rule,* pp. 21–23.

47. Karl, "Dilemmas of Democratization," p. 9.

48. Ibid., p. 8.

49. Terry Lynn Karl and Philippe C. Schmitter, "Modes of Transition in Latin America, Southern and Eastern Europe," *International Social Science Journal* 128 (1991): 269–284.

50. Linz, "Transitions to Democracy," p. 158.

51. Ibid.

52. Jose Nun, "Democracy and Modernization, Thirty Years After" (Paper delivered at the XVth World Congress of the International Political Science Association, Buenos Aires, July 21–25, 1991), p. 23.

53. For a case study, see Thomas R. Rochon and Michael J. Mitchell, "Cultural Components of the Consolidation of Democracy in Brazil" (Paper delivered at the annual meeting of the American Political Science Association, Washington, D.C., August 28–31, 1991).

54. Some of what follows draws on Georg Sørensen, "Democracy and the Developmental State" (Institute of Political Science, University of Aarhus, 1991, Mimeographed).

55. See Frances Hagopian, "'Democracy by Undemocratic Means?' Elites, Political Pacts, and Regime Transition in Brazil," *Comparative Political Studies* 23, no. 2 (1990): 154–157.

56. Ibid., p. 157.

57. Ibid., p. 159.

58. See Karl, "Dilemmas of Democratization," p. 14.

59. For a case study of the Chilean transition, see Hans-Jørgen Nielsen, *Den Chilenske Transitionsproces* (The Chilean process of transition) (Aarhus: University of Aarhus, Institute of Political Science, 1991).

60. This argument is made by O'Donnell and Schmitter, *Transitions from Authoritarian Rule*, p. 66.

61. Karl, "Dilemmas of Democratization," p. 13.

62. See Juan Rial, "Transitions in Latin America on the Threshold of the 1990s," *International Social Science Journal* 128 (1991): 299; Carlos H. Waisman, "Argentina: Autarkic Industrialization and Illegitimacy," in Larry Diamond, Juan J. Linz, and Seymour Martin Lipset (eds.), *Democracy in Developing Countries*. Vol. 4: *Latin America* (Boulder: Lynne Rienner, 1989), p. 102.

63. Rial, "Transitions in Latin America," p. 290.

64. Karl, "Dilemmas of Democratization," p. 12.

65. Dahl, *Polyarchy*, p. 50.

66. World Bank, *Sub-Saharan Africa: From Crisis to Sustainable Growth. A Long-Term Perspective Study* (Washington, D.C.: World Bank, 1989), p. 1.

67. Some of what follows draws on Sørensen, "Democracy and the Developmental State."

68. Richard Sandbrook, *The Politics of Africa's Economic Stagnation* (Cambridge: Cambridge University Press, 1985); Richard Sandbrook, "The State and Economic Stagnation in Tropical Africa," *World Development* 14, no. 3 (1986): 319–332; Goran Hyden, *No Shortcuts to Progress: African Development Management in Perspective* (London: Heinemann, 1983); Robert Jackson and Carl G. Rosberg, *Personal Rule in Black Africa: Prince, Autocrat, Prophet, Tyrant* (Berkeley: University of California Press, 1982).

69. Sandbrook, "The State and Economic Stagnation," p. 324.

70. Ibid.

71. Ruth Berins Collier, *Regimes in Tropical Africa: Changing Forms of Supremacy 1945–75* (Berkeley: University of California Press, 1975), p. 22.

72. See, for example, Robert Jackson and Carl G. Rosberg, "Democracy in Tropical Africa: Democracy Versus Autocracy in African Politics," *Journal of International Affairs* 38, no. 2 (1985): 305.

73. Ibid., p. 301.

74. Linz, "Transitions to Democracy," p. 146.

75. See Marina Ottaway, "Democratization in Collapsed States," in William I. Zartmann (ed.), *Collapsed States. The Disintegration and Restoration of Legitimate Authority* (Boulder: Lynne Rienner, 1995), pp. 235–251.

76. Robert A. Dahl, *Democracy and Its Critics* (New Haven: Yale University Press, 1989), p. 314.

77. For a case study of Botswana, see John D. Holm, "Botswana: A Paternalistic Democracy," in Diamond, Linz, and Lipset (eds.), *Democracy in Developing Countries*, Vol. 2, pp. 179–217.

78. Quoted from Timothy Garton Ash, *The Polish Revolution* (London: Hodder & Stoughton, 1985), p. 1.

79. Janos Kis, "Turning Point in Hungary," *Dissent* (Spring 1989): 238.

80. See Ole Nørgaard, "Reflections on the Revolutions in Eastern Europe" (Institute of Political Science, University of Aarhus, 1990, Mimeographed).

81. "A valley of tears" is an expression used by Ralf Dahrendorf in a lecture on Eastern Europe in Oslo, 1990.

82. Nørgaard, "De post-stalinistiske samfund," and Paul G. Lewis, "Democratization in Eastern Europe," Coexistence 27 (1990): 245–267.

83. Karl and Schmitter, "Modes of Transition," p. 272.

84. Przeworski, "The 'East' Becomes the 'South'?" p. 23n.

85. See Linz, "Transitions to Democracy," p. 152.

86. O'Donnell and Schmitter, Transitions from Authoritarian Rule, p. 54.

87. David Lehmann, Democracy and Development in Latin America (Cambridge: Polity Press, 1990), p. 150.

88. Naomi Chazan, "The New Politics of Participation in Tropical Africa," Comparative Politics 14, no. 2 (1982): 172.

89. Sandbrook, The Politics of Africa's Economic Stagnation, p. 148.

90. Sandbrook, "Liberal Democracy in Africa," p. 262.

91. Rochon and Mitchell, "Cultural Components," p. 17.

92. Ralf Dahrendorf, lecture on Eastern Europe, Oslo, 1990.

93. Karl, "Dilemmas of Democratization," p. 17.

94. Douglas W. Payne, "Latin America and the Caribbean: Storm Warnings," in Roger Kaplan et al. (eds.), Freedom in the World. The Annual Survey of Political Rights and Civil Liberties 1995–1996 (New York: Freedom House, 1996).

95. The Economist 341 (7994): 24.

96. Anne Applebaum, "Central Europe: Nice Guys Finish Last," in Roger Kaplan et al. (eds.), Freedom in the World. The Annual Survey of Political Rights and Civil Liberties 1995–1996 (New York: Freedom House, 1996).

97. Loc. cit.

Chapter Three

1. For a recent overview of the debate, see Larry Sirowy and Alex Inkeles, "The Effects of Democracy on Economic Growth and Inequality: A Review," Studies in Comparative International Development 25, no. 1 (1990): 126–157. Some of what follows draws on Georg Sørensen, Democracy, Dictatorship and Development: Economic Development in Selected Regimes of the Third World (London: Macmillan, 1991).

2. B. K. Nehru, "Western Democracy and the Third World," Third World Quarterly 1, no. 2 (1979): p. 57n. See also V. Rao, "Democracy and Economic Development," Studies in Comparative International Development 19, no. 4 (1984–1985): 67–82.

3. Samuel P. Huntington, Political Order in Changing Societies (New Haven: Yale University Press, 1968).

4. David E. Apter, The Politics of Modernization (Chicago: University of Chicago Press, 1965).

5. See Dieter Senghaas, The European Experience: A Historical Critique of Development Theory (Leamington Spa/Dover: Berg Publishers, 1985), and Dieter Seng-

haas, "China 1979," in J. Habermas (ed.), *Stichworte zur "Geistigen Situation der Zeit,"* Vol. 1 (Frankfurt Main: Suhrkamp, 1979), p. 435.

6. J. A. Hall, *Powers and Liberties: The Causes and Consequences of the Rise of the West* (Harmondsworth: Penguin, 1986), p. 222.

7. Gabriel Almond and G. Bingham Powell, *Comparative Politics: A Developmental Approach* (Boston: Little, Brown, 1978), p. 363. See also Samuel P. Huntington, "The Goals of Development," in Myron Weiner and Samuel P. Huntington (eds.), *Understanding Political Development* (Boston: Little, Brown, 1987), p. 19, and Irene Gendzier, *Managing Political Change: Social Scientists and the Third World* (Boulder: Westview, 1985), ch. 6.

8. See Hollis Chenery et al., *Redistribution with Growth* (London: Oxford University Press, 1974), and Paul Streeten et al., *First Things First: Meeting Basic Human Needs in Developing Countries* (New York: Oxford University Press, 1981).

9. See Grace Goodell and John P. Powelson, "The Democratic Prerequisites of Development," in Raymond Gastil (ed.), *Freedom in the World: Political Rights and Civil Liberties* (New York: Freedom House, 1982), pp. 167–176, and Atul Kohli, "Democracy and Development," in John Lewis and Valeriana Kallab (eds.), *Development Strategies Reconsidered* (New Brunswick, N.J.: Transaction Books, 1986), pp. 153–182.

10. Richard Claude, "The Classical Model of Human Rights Development," in Richard Claude (ed.), *Comparative Human Rights* (Baltimore: Johns Hopkins University Press, 1976), pp. 6–50.

11. See Georg Sørensen, "Democracy and the Developmental State" (Institute of Political Science, University of Aarhus, 1991. Mimeographed).

12. See the overview in Sirowy and Inkeles, "The Effects of Democracy on Economic Growth."

13. Robert M. Marsh, "Does Democracy Hinder Economic Development in the Latecomer Developing Nations?" *Comparative Social Research* 2 (1979): 244.

14. Yousseff Cohen, "The Impact of Bureaucratic-Authoritarian Rule on Economic Growth," *Comparative Political Studies* 18, no. 1 (1985): 123–136.

15. Dirk Berg-Schlosser, "African Political Systems: Typology and Performance," *Comparative Political Studies* 17, no. 1 (1984): 143.

16. Ibid., p. 121.

17. Dwight Y. King, "Regime Type and Performance: Authoritarian Rule, Semi-Capitalist Development and Rural Inequality in Asia," *Comparative Political Studies* 13, no. 4 (1981): 477.

18. G. William Dick, "Authoritarian Versus Nonauthoritarian Approaches to Economic Development," *Journal of Political Economy* 82, no. 4 (1974): 823.

19. Sirowy and Inkeles, "The Effects of Democracy on Economic Growth."

20. Some of these considerations draw on Sørensen, *Democracy, Dictatorship and Development.*

21. See Jean Drèze and Amartya Sen, *Hunger and Public Action* (Oxford: Clarendon Press, 1989), p. 206n.

22. See C. Ka and M. Selden, "Original Accumulation, Equity and Late Industrialization: The Cases of Socialist China and Capitalist Taiwan," *World Development* 14, no. 10/11 (1986): 1300n.

23. See, for example, Francine Frankel, "Is Authoritarianism the Solution to India's Economic Development Problems?" in Atul Kohli (ed.), *The State and Development in the Third World* (Princeton: Princeton University Press, 1986), pp. 154–161.

24. Barrington Moore, Jr., *Social Origins of Dictatorship and Democracy: Lord and Peasant in the Making of the Modern World* (Boston: Beacon Press, 1966), p. 355.

25. Pranab Bardhan, *The Political Economy of Development in India* (Delhi: Oxford University Press, 1984), p. 56. See also Rajni Kothari, *Politics in India* (Delhi: Orient Longman, 1982), p. 352n, and K. Subbarao, "State Policies and Regional Disparity in Indian Agriculture," *Development and Change* 16, no. 4 (1985): 543.

26. A. Piazza, *Food Consumption and Nutritional Status in the PRC* (Boulder: Westview, 1986), p. 36.

27. Carl Riskin, *China's Political Economy: The Quest for Development Since 1949* (Oxford: Oxford University Press, 1987), p. 276.

28. See Ka and Selden, "Original Accumulation," p. 1301.

29. Clemens Stubbe Østergaard and Christina Petersen, "Official Profiteering and the Tiananmen Square Demonstrations in China" (Paper delivered at the Second Liverpool Conference on Fraud, Corruption and Business Crime, Liverpool, April 17–19, 1991).

30. See Sørensen, *Democracy, Dictatorship and Development.*

31. G. Etienne, *India's Changing Rural Scene 1963–79* (New Delhi: Oxford University Press, 1982), pp. 152–158; J. Breman, "I Am the Government Labour Officer . . . State Protection for Rural Proletariat of South Gujarat," *Economic and Political Weekly* 20, no. 4 (June 15, 1985): 1043–1056.

32. Bardhan, *The Political Economy of Development in India*, p. 4.

33. The following analysis draws heavily on Bardhan, *The Political Economy of Development in India.*

34. See A. Rudra, "Political Economy of Indian Non-Development," *Economic and Political Weekly* 20, no. 21 (May 25, 1985), p. 916.

35. Riskin, *China's Political Economy*, p. 235.

36. See Piazza, *Food Consumption and Nutritional Status*, p. 176.

37. Drèze and Sen, *Hunger and Public Action*, p. 209.

38. Ibid., p. 215.

39. See, for example, Thomas B. Gold, *State and Society in the Taiwan Miracle* (New York: M. E. Sharpe, 1986).

40. Jon Halliday, "The North Korean Enigma," in Gordon White et al. (eds.), *Revolutionary Socialist Development in the Third World* (Brighton: Wheatsheaf, 1983), pp. 114–155; Clive Hamilton, *Capitalist Industrialization in Korea* (Boulder: Westview, 1986).

41. Peter T. Knight, "Brazilian Socio-Economic Development: Issues for the Eighties," *World Development* 9, no. 11–12 (1981).

42. Sylvia Ann Hewlett, *The Cruel Dilemmas of Development: Twentieth Century Brazil* (New York: Basic Books, 1980).

43. See C. Ominami, "Déindustrialisation et restructuration industrielle en Argentine, au Brésil et au Chili," *Problemas D'Amerique Latine* 89 (1988): 55–79.

44. D. Cruise O'Brien, quoted from Goran Hyden, *No Shortcuts to Progress: African Development Management in Perspective* (London: Heineman, 1983), p. 37.

45. David Gould, "The Administration of Underdevelopment," in Guy Gran (ed.), *Zaire: The Political Economy of Underdevelopment* (New York: Praeger, 1979), pp. 87–107; Salua Nour, "Zaire," in Dieter Nohlen and Franz Nuscheler (eds.), *Handbuch der Dritten Welt*, Vol. 4 (Hamburg: Hoffmann und Campe), pp. 468–522.

46. Nour, "Zaire," p. 512.

47. See Hewlett, *The Cruel Dilemmas of Development*, and Knight, "Brazilian Socio-Economic Development."

48. See Sørensen, *Democracy, Dictatorship and Development*, ch. 2.

49. See Charles D. Ameringer, *Democracy in Costa Rica* (New York: Praeger, 1982); John A. Peeler, *Latin American Democracies: Colombia, Costa Rica, Venezuela* (Chapel Hill: University of North Carolina Press, 1985).

50. Peeler, *Latin American Democracies*, p. 129.

51. See C. Hall, *Costa Rica: A Geographical Interpretation in Historical Perspective* (Boulder: Westview, 1985), p. 270.

52. Ameringer, *Democracy in Costa Rica*, p. 19.

53. J. A. Booth, "Costa Rica," in Larry Diamond, Juan J. Linz, and Seymour Martin Lipset (eds.), *Democracy in Developing Countries*. Vol. 4: *Latin America* (Boulder: Lynne Rienner, 1989), p. 417.

54. The remarks on Chile are based on Jakob J. Simonsen and Georg Sørensen, *Chile 1970–73: Et eksempel på Østeuropæisk udviklingsstrategi?* (Aarhus: University of Aarhus, Institute of Political Science, 1976).

55. See Atul Kohli, *The State and Poverty in India: The Politics of Reform* (Cambridge, Mass.: Harvard University Press, 1987).

56. Stephan Haggard and Robert R. Kaufman, *The Political Economy of Democratic Transitions* (Princeton: Princeton University Press, 1995). The following remarks are based on this contribution.

57. Ibid., p. 227.

58. Ibid., p. 370.

59. Ibid., p. 371.

60. Jack Donnelly, "Human Rights and Development: Complementary or Competing Concerns?" *World Politics* 36, no. 2 (1984): 281n.

61. See, for example, Johan Galtung, "Why the Concern with Ways of Life?" in Council for International Development Studies, *The Western Development Model and Life Style* (Oslo: University of Oslo, 1980).

62. See Jack Donnelly, *Human Rights and World Politics* (Boulder: Westview, 1993).

63. United Nations Development Programme (UNDP), *Human Development Report 1991* (New York: Oxford University Press, 1991), p. 20.

64. See Richard Falk, *Human Rights and State Sovereignty* (New York: Holmes and Meier, 1981), pp. 63–124.

65. See Stephen Marks, "Promoting Human Rights," in Michael T. Klare and Daniel C. Thomas, *World Security: Trends and Challenges at Century's End* (New York: St. Martin's Press, 1991), p. 303.

Chapter Four

1. An English version of Kant's "Perpetual Peace" can be found in Hans Reiss (ed.), *Kant's Political Writings* (Cambridge: Cambridge University Press, 1970). My summary of Kant's ideas relies heavily on three articles by Michael W. Doyle: "Kant, Liberal Legacies and Foreign Affairs," *Philosophy and Public Affairs* 12, no. 3 (1983): 205–235; "Kant, Liberal Legacies and Foreign Affairs, Part 2," *Philosophy and Public Affairs* 12, no. 4 (1983): 323–354; and "Liberalism and World Politics," *American Political Science Review* 80, no. 4 (1986): 1151–1169.

2. Quoted from Reiss, *Kant's Political Writings*, p. 100.

3. Quoted from Doyle, "Liberalism and World Politics," p. 1153.

4. See Rudolph J. Rummel, "Libertarianism and International Violence," *Journal of Conflict Resolution* 27, no. 1 (1983): 27–71.

5. See Melvin Small and J. David Singer, "The War-Proneness of Democratic Regimes," *The Jerusalem Journal of International Relations* 1, no. 4 (1976): 50–69; Steve Chan, "Mirror, Mirror on the Wall . . . Are the Freer Countries More Pacific?" *Journal of Conflict Resolution* 28, no. 4 (1984): 617–648; Erich Weede, "Democracy and War Involvement," *Journal of Conflict Resolution* 28, no. 4 (1984): 649–664. Yet it should be added that studies such as Chan's (cited in note 5), which are based on very long periods of observation, face other difficulties because, as was demonstrated in Chapter 1, the concrete content of the entity called "democracy" changes over time.

6. Doyle, "Kant, Liberal Legacies and Foreign Affairs," p. 213.

7. Dean Babst, "Elective Governments—A Force for Peace," *The Wisconsin Sociologist* 3, no. 1 (1964): 9–14; see also Small and Singer, "The War-Proneness of Democratic Regimes"; Chan, "Mirror, Mirror"; Bruce Russett, "Democracy and Peace," in B. Russett, H. Starr, and R. J. Stoll, *Choices in World Politics: Sovereignty and Interdependence* (New York: Freeman and Company, 1989), pp. 245–261; and James Lee Ray, "The Future of International War" (Paper delivered at the Annual Meeting of the American Political Science Association, Washington, D.C., August 29 to September 1, 1991).

8. Russett, "Democracy and Peace," p. 245.

9. Reiss, *Kant's Political Writings*, p. 114.

10. Doyle, "Liberalism and World Politics," p. 1161.

11. Doyle, "Kant, Liberal Legacies and Foreign Affairs, Part 2," p. 324n. This quotation was italicized in the original.

12. See Russett, "Democracy and Peace," p. 250.

13. Walter Lippmann, *Essays in the Public Philosophy* (Boston: Little, Brown, 1955), p. 20.

14. Doyle, "Kant, Liberal Legacies and Foreign Affairs, Part 2," p. 344.

15. Quoted from Kjell Goldmann, "'Democracy Is Incompatible with International Politics': Reconsideration of a Hypothesis," in K. Goldmann, S. Berglund, and G. Sjöstedt, *Democracy and Foreign Policy* (Aldershot: Gower, 1986), p. 2.

16. Ibid. There are several modern versions of Ponsonby's argument. See, for example, Jørgen Christensen, *Demokratiet og sikkerhedspolitikken*, Vols. I and II (Democracy and security policy) (Aarhus: University of Aarhus, Institute of Political Science, 1990).

17. See Goldmann, "'Democracy Is Incompatible with International Politics,'" pp. 5–8.

18. Ibid., p. 7n.

19. Further distinctions have been made that focus the argument concerning incompatibility primarily on diplomatic security policy. They are outlined in ibid., pp. 27–31.

20. Thomas Risse-Kappen, "Public Opinion, Domestic Structure, and Foreign Policy in Liberal Democracies," World Politics 43, no. 4 (1991): 479–513.

21. Ibid., p. 510.

22. Bruce Russett and Harvey Starr, World Politics: The Menu for Choice (New York: W. H. Freeman, 1985), p. 250. See also Hans-Henrik Holm, "The Democratic Victory: What Will Happen to Foreign Policy?" in Wojtech Kostecki (ed.), Eastern Europe in Transition: A Chance or Threat to Peace? Proceedings of a seminar (Warsaw: Polish Institute of International Affairs, 1991), pp. 44–63; and Kurt Taylor Gaubatz, "Election Cycles and War," Journal of Conflict Resolution 35, no. 2 (1991): 212–245.

23. Doyle, "Kant, Liberal Legacies and Foreign Affairs," p. 213.

24. See Stephen Van Evera, "Primed for Peace: Europe After the Cold War," International Security 15, no. 3 (1990/1991): 26n.

25. Ibid., p. 25.

26. Doyle, "Kant, Liberal Legacies and Foreign Affairs," p. 213; Russett, "Democracy and Peace," p. 260.

27. Some of what follows draws on Georg Sørensen, "Individual Security and National Security. The State Remains the Principal Problem," Security Dialogue 27, no. 4 (1996): 371–386.

28. Marina Ottaway, "Democratization in Collapsed States," in William I. Zartmann (ed.), Collapsed States. The Disintegration and Restoration of Legitimate Authority (Boulder: Lynne Rienner, 1995), p. 243.

29. Adam Watson, "European International Society and Its Expansion," in Hedley Bull and Adam Watson (eds.), The Expansion of International Society (Oxford: Clarendon Press, 1988), p. 23.

30. Ibid., p. 24n.

31. Ibid., p. 1.

32. Barry Buzan, People, States and Fear: An Agenda for International Security Studies in the Post-Cold War Era (Hemel Hempstead: Harvester Wheatsheaf, 1991), p. 169.

33. Daniel Bell, The Coming of Post-Industrial Society: A Venture in Social Forecasting (New York: Basic Books, 1973), p. 317.

34. See, for example, James N. Rosenau, Turbulence in World Politics: A Theory of Change and Continuity (Princeton: Princeton University Press, 1990), pp. 416–443.

35. See Barry Buzan, "New Patterns of Global Security in the Twenty-First Century," International Affairs 67, no. 3 (1991): 431–451.

36. See Karl Deutsch and S. A. Burrell, Political Community and the North Atlantic Area (Princeton: Princeton University Press, 1957). See also Buzan, "New Patterns of Global Security," p. 436.

37. See Volker Rittberger, "Zur Friedensfähigkeit von Demokratien," *Aus Politik und Zeitgeschichte,* no. 44 (1987): 3–12. Today (1997), Greece is a political democracy but Turkey is not; therefore, the continuing conflict between the two countries is not a conflict between democracies.

38. Speech printed in the *New York Times,* March 12, 1913, p. 1, quoted from Cole Blasier, "The United States and Democracy in Latin America," in James M. Malloy and Mitchell A. Seligson (eds.), *Authoritarians and Democrats: Regime Transition in Latin America* (Pittsburgh: University of Pittsburgh Press, 1987), pp. 219–233.

39. Quoted from Doyle, "Kant, Liberal Legacies and Foreign Affairs, Part 2," p. 335.

40. See, for example, James Petras and Morris Morley, *How Allende Fell* (Nottingham: Spokesman, 1974).

41. On U.S. involvement in Central America, see Thomas Carothers, *In the Name of Democracy: U.S. Policy Toward Latin America in the Reagan Years* (Los Angeles: University of California Press, 1991).

42. Russett, "Democracy and Peace," p. 256.

43. See Aldo C. Vacs, "Ambiguous Crusade, Uncertain Commitment: International Factors and the Transition to Democracy in the 1980s" (Paper delivered at the XVth World Congress of the International Political Science Association, Buenos Aires, July 21–25, 1991). See also Richard Sandbrook, "Taming the African Leviathan," *World Policy Journal 7,* no. 4 (1990): 673–701.

44. See Timothy Garton Ash, "Ten Thoughts on the New Europe," *The New York Review of Books,* June 14, 1990; the Dienstbier quotation is from page 22 of this article.

45. Alex Inkeles, "The Emerging Social Structure of the World," *World Politics* 27, no. 4 (1975): 479.

46. See Barry B. Hughes, *Continuity and Change in World Politics* (Englewood Cliffs, N.J.: Prentice-Hall, 1991), p. 328n. For the view that the growth of trade and investment should not be exaggerated relative to the levels in the early twentieth century, see Janice E. Thompson and Stephen D. Krasner, "Global Transactions and the Consolidation of Sovereignty," in E-O. Czempiel and J. Rosenau (eds.), *Global Changes and Theoretical Challenges* (Lexington, Mass.: Lexington Books, 1989), pp. 195–220.

47. See Stephen D. Krasner, "State Power and the Structure of International Trade," *World Politics* 28, no. 3 (1976): 317–348.

48. Deutsch and Burrell, *Political Community,* p. 5.

49. See, for example, Frederic C. Deyo (ed.), *The Political Economy of the New Asian Industrialism* (Ithaca: Cornell University Press, 1987).

50. See, for example, J. Galtung, P. O'Brien, and R. Preiswerk (eds.), *Self-Reliance: A Strategy for Development* (London: Bogle-L'Overture, 1980).

51. For the changes in strategy, see Georg Sørensen, "Strategies and Structures of Development: The New 'Consensus' and the Limits to Its Promises," *European Journal of Development Research* 3, no. 2 (1991): 121–146. For a discussion of the shrinking market opportunities and other problems for the South, see John

Ravenhill, "The North-South Balance of Power," *International Affairs* 66, no. 4 (1990): 731–748.

52. Joan Edelman Spero, *The Politics of International Economic Relations* (London: George Allen & Unwin, 1985), p. 169n.

53. See Walden Bello and Stephanie Rosenfeld, "Dragons in Distress: The Crisis of the NICs," *World Policy Journal 7*, no. 3 (1990): 431–469.

54. See Sandbrook, "Taming the African Leviathan," and John Ravenhill, "Reversing Africa's Economic Decline: No Easy Answers," *World Policy Journal 7*, no. 4 (1990): 703–732. For discussion of the debt crisis in Latin America, see David Felix, "Latin America's Debt Crisis," *World Policy Journal 7*, no. 4 (1990): 733–771. The quote is from World Bank, *Sub-Saharan Africa: From Crisis to Sustainable Growth* (Washington, D.C.: World Bank, 1989), p. 185.

55. John J. Mearsheimer, "Back to the Future: Instability in Europe After the Cold War," *International Security* 15, no. 1 (1990): 49.

56. Ibid., pp. 49–51.

57. Ibid., p. 50.

58. Buzan, *People, States and Fear,* p. 190.

59. The argument is set forth at length on a neorealist basis in ibid., pp. 186–229.

60. Ole Wæver, "Conflicts of Vision: Visions of Conflict," in Ole Wæver et al. (eds.), *European Polyphony: Perspectives Beyond East-West Confrontation* (London: Macmillan, 1989), pp. 283–327. For a theoretical argument in favor of different forms of anarchy, see Alexander Wendt, "Anarchy Is What States Make of It: The Social Construction of Power Politics," *International Organization* 46, no. 2 (1992): 391–425.

61. Robert Jervis, "Security Regimes," *International Organization* 36, no. 2 (1982): 357.

62. Mearsheimer, "Back to the Future," p. 50.

63. The continuing debate on democracy and peace can be followed in the professional journals, especially *International Security* and *Journal of Peace Research.*

Chapter Five

1. Francis Fukuyama, "The End of History?" *The National Interest*, no. 16 (1989): 4.

2. Samuel P. Huntington, "Democracy's Third Wave," *Journal of Democracy* 2, no. 2 (1991): 33. See also Samuel P. Huntington, "No Exit: The Errors of Endism," *The National Interest*, no. 17 (1989): 3–11.

3. For an example of how the debate continues and the many unanswered questions, see "Roundtable Discussion: Politics, Economics, and Welfare," in Ian Shapiro and Grant Reeher (eds.), *Power, Inequality, and Democratic Politics: Essays in Honor of Robert A. Dahl* (Boulder: Westview, 1988), pp. 153–167.

4. Robert C. Johansen, "A Policy Framework for World Security," in Michael T. Klare and Daniel C. Thomas, *World Security: Trends and Challenges at Century's End* (New York: St. Martin's Press, 1991), p. 412.

5. Richard Falk, *Human Rights and State Sovereignty* (New York: Holmes & Meier, 1981), p. 103.

6. David Held, *Models of Democracy* (Cambridge: Polity Press, 1987), pp. 267–301.

7. UN Centre on Transnational Corporations, *Transnational Corporations in World Development* (New York: United Nations, 1988), p. 92.

8. Pascal Bruckner, *La mélancolie démocratique* (Paris: Editions du Seuil, 1990); Oliver Mongin, *La peur du vide* (Paris: Editions du Seuil, 1990).

9. See Neal Ascherson, "Old Wounds Exposed by Post-Communist Thaw," *The Independent*, October 6, 1991.

10. Robert A. Dahl, *Democracy and Its Critics* (New Haven: Yale University Press, 1989), p. 314. The conditions outlined by Dahl were set forth in Chapter 2 of this volume.

11. Ibid., p. 315.

12. Huntington, "Democracy's Third Wave," p. 21.

13. Ibid., p. 33.

14. Dahl's quote appears in *Democracy and Its Critics*, p. 313.

15. Francisco C. Weffort, "A America errada," *Lua Nova* 21 (1990): 39.

16. Timothy Garton Ash, "Eastern Europe: The Year of Truth," *The New York Review of Books*, February 15, 1990, p. 21.

17. See, for example, Rebekka Sylvest, *Værdier og udvikling i Saudi-Arabien* (Values and development in Saudi Arabia) (Aarhus: University of Aarhus, Institute of Political Science, 1991). For the role of Islam as a carrier of anti-Western sentiment, see Barry Buzan, "New Patterns of Global Security in the Twenty-First Century," *International Affairs* 67, no. 3 (1991): 441n.

18. Ghia Nadia, "How Different are Postcommunist Transitions," *Journal of Democracy* 7, no. 4 (1996): 15–29.

19. Larry Diamond, "Is the Third Wave Over?" *Journal of Democracy* 7, no. 3 (1996): 20–38. The countries in the lower end of the "free" category are also in need of further democratic progress; they have some of the same problems as the "electoral democracies."

20. Ibid., p. 28.

21. Adam Przeworski et al., "What Makes Democracies Endure?" *Journal of Democracy* 7, no. 1 (1996): 49.

22. The following remarks draw on Larry Diamond, "Is the Third Wave Over?"; Scott Mainwaring and Timothy R. Scully (eds.), *Building Democratic Institutions. Party Systems in Latin America* (Stanford: Stanford University Press, 1995); Seymour Martin Lipset, "The Social Requisites of Democracy Revisited," *American Sociological Review* 59 (February 1994): 1–22; and Arend Lijphart and Carlos H. Waisman (eds.), *Institutional Design in New Democracies: Eastern Europe and Latin America* (Boulder: Westview, 1996).

23. Lijphart and Waisman, *Institutional Design in New Democracies*, p. 236.

24. Ibid.

25. See Lipset, "The Social Requisites of Democracy Revisited."

26. Mainwaring and Scully, *Building Democratic Institutions*, p. 27.

27. Ibid., p. 5. Mainwaring and Scully identify four conditions for institutionalization: (1) the rules and the nature of interparty competition are both stable; (2) parties have somewhat stable roots in society; (3) the major political actors accord

legitimacy to the electoral process and to parties; and (4) party organizations play an independent role in the political process and are not under the complete control of powerful leaders.

28. Robert D. Putnam, *Making Democracy Work. Civic Traditions in Modern Italy* (Princeton: Princeton University Press, 1993); see also Robert D. Putnam, "Bowling Alone: America's Declining Social Capital," *Journal of Democracy* 5, no. 1 (1995): 65–78.

29. See Sidney Tarrow, "Making Social Science Work Across Space and Time: A Critical Reflection on Robert Putnam's *Making Democracy Work,*" *American Political Science Review* 90, no. 2 (1995): 389–397.

30. For this argument, see Paul Hirst and Grahame Thompson, *Globalization in Question: The International Economy and the Possibilities of Government* (Cambridge: Polity Press, 1996).

31. See, for example, Philip G. Cerny, "Globalisation and the Erosion of Democracy," Paper for ECPR workshop, Berne 1997; and David Held, *Democracy and the Global Order* (Cambridge: Polity Press, 1995).

32. Robert O. Keohane and Helen V. Milner (eds.), *Internationalization and Domestic Politics* (Cambridge: Cambridge University Press, 1996), p. 256.

33. Held, *Democracy and the Global Order,* p. 232.

34. Ibid., p. 233.

□ □ □

Suggested Readings

Ake, Claude. *Democracy and Development in Africa*. Washington, D.C.: Brookings Institution, 1996.

Ash, Timothy Garton. *In Europe's Name. Germany and the Divided Continent*. London: Vintage, 1994.

Bardhan, Pranab. *The Political Economy of Development in India*. Delhi: Oxford University Press, 1984.

Bull, Hedley, and Adam Watson (eds.). *The Expansion of International Society*. Oxford: Clarendon Press, 1988.

Carothers, Thomas. *In the Name of Democracy: U.S. Policy Toward Latin America in the Reagan Years*. Los Angeles: University of California Press, 1991.

Chan, Steve. "Mirror, Mirror on the Wall . . . Are the Freer Countries More Pacific?" *Journal of Conflict Resolution* 28, no. 4 (1984): 617–648.

Cohen, Yousseff. "The Impact of Bureaucratic-Authoritarian Rule on Economic Growth." *Comparative Political Studies* 18, no. 1 (1985): 123–136.

Dahl, Robert A. *Polyarchy: Participation and Opposition*. New Haven: Yale University Press, 1971.

_____. *Democracy and Its Critics*. New Haven: Yale University Press, 1989.

Diamond, Larry (ed.). *Political Culture & Democracy in Developing Countries*. Boulder: Lynne Rienner, 1994.

Diamond, Larry, Juan J. Linz, and Seymour Martin Lipset (eds.). *Democracy in Developing Countries*. Vol. 1: *Persistence, Failure, and Renewal*. Vol. 2: *Africa*. Vol. 3: *Asia*. Vol. 4: *Latin America*. Boulder: Lynne Rienner, 1988, 1989.

Diamond, Larry, and M. F. Plattner (eds.). *The Global Resurgence of Democracy*. Baltimore: Johns Hopkins University Press, 1993.

Donnelly, Jack. "Human Rights and Development: Complementary or Competing Concerns?" *World Politics* 36, no. 2 (1984): 255–284.

_____. *International Human Rights*. Boulder: Westview, 1993.

Doyle, Michael W. "Kant, Liberal Legacies and Foreign Affairs." *Philosophy and Public Affairs* 12, no. 3 (1983): 205–235.

Elklit, Jørgen, and Palle Svensson. "Kant, Liberal Legacies and Foreign Affairs, Part 2." *Philosophy and Public Affairs* 12, no. 4 (1983): 323–354.

_____. "Liberalism and World Politics." *American Political Science Review* 80, no. 4 (1986): 1151–1169.

_____. "When are Elections Free and Fair—Or at Least Acceptable?" *Journal of Democracy* 8, no. 3 (1997).

155

Frankel, Francine. "Is Authoritarianism the Solution to India's Economic Development Problems?" In Atul Kohli (ed.), *The State and Development in the Third World*. Princeton: Princeton University Press, 1986, pp. 154–161.

Fukuyama, Francis. "The End of History?" *The National Interest*, no. 16 (1989): 3–18.

Gills, Barry et al. (eds.). "The Developmental State?: Democracy, Reform and Economic Prosperity in the Third World in the Nineties." Special Issue, *Third World Quarterly* 17, no. 4 (1996), pp. 585–855.

Goldmann, Kjell. " 'Democracy Is Incompatible with International Politics': Reconsideration of a Hypothesis." In K. Goldmann, S. Berglund, and G. Sjostedt, *Democracy and Foreign Policy*. Aldershot: Gower, 1986, pp. 1–44.

Haggard, Stephan, and Robert R. Kaufman. *The Political Economy of Democratic Transitions*. Princeton: Princeton University Press, 1995.

Haggard, Stephan, and Robert R. Kaufman (eds.). *The Politics of Economic Adjustment*. Princeton: Princeton University Press, 1992.

Held, David. *Models of Democracy*. Cambridge: Polity Press, 1987.

_____. *Prospects for Democracy. North, South, East, West*. Stanford: Stanford University Press, 1993.

_____. *Democracy and the Global Order. From the Modern State to Cosmopolitan Governance*. Cambridge: Polity Press, 1995.

Holm, Hans-Henrik. "The Democratic Victory: What Will Happen to Foreign Policy?" In Wojtech Kostecki (ed.), *Eastern Europe in Transition: A Chance or Threat to Peace*? Proceedings of a seminar (Warsaw: Polish Institute of International Affairs, 1991), pp. 44–63.

Huntington, Samuel P. "Will More Countries Become Democratic?" *Political Science Quarterly* 99, no. 2 (1984): 193–218.

_____. "No Exit: The Errors of Endism." *The National Interest*, no. 17 (1989): 3–11.

_____. *The Third Wave: Democratization in the Late Twentieth Century*. Norman: University of Oklahoma Press, 1991.

Hyden, Goran. *No Shortcuts to Progress: African Development Management in Perspective*. London: Heinemann, 1983.

Jackson, Robert, and Carl G. Rosberg. *Personal Rule in Black Africa: Prince, Autocrat, Prophet, Tyrant*. Berkeley: University of California Press, 1982.

Journal of Democracy. This quarterly journal provides wide coverage of current processes of democratization as well as in-depth background analyses.

Karl, Terry Lynn. "Dilemmas of Democratization in Latin America." *Comparative Politics* 23, no. 1 (1990): 1–21.

King, Dwight Y. "Regime Type and Performance: Authoritarian Rule, Semi-Capitalist Development and Rural Inequality in Asia." *Comparative Political Studies* 13, no. 4 (1981): 477–504.

Kohli, Atul. "Democracy and Development." In John Lewis and Valeriana Kallab (eds.), *Development Strategies Reconsidered*. New Brunswick, N.J.: Transaction Books, 1986, pp. 153–182.

Lee Ray, James. *Democracy and International Conflict: An Evaluation of the Democratic Peace Proposition*. Columbia University of South Carolina Press, 1995.

Lewis, Paul G. "Democratization in Eastern Europe." *Coexistence* 27 (1990): 245–267.

Linz, Juan J. "Transitions to Democracy." *The Washington Quarterly* 13, no. 3 (1990): 143–164.

Lipset, Seymour Martin (ed.). *The Encyclopedia of Democracy.* Washington, D.C.: Congressional Quarterly, and London: Routledge, 1995. Four volumes.

Macpherson, C. B. *The Life and Times of Liberal Democracy.* Oxford: Oxford University Press, 1977.

Mansfield, Edward, and Jack Snyder. "Democratization and War." *International Security* 20, no. 1 (1995): 5–38.

Marsh, Rodney M. "Does Democracy Hinder Economic Development in the Latecomer Developing Nations?" *Comparative Social Research* 2 (1979): 215–248.

Mearsheimer, John J. "Back to the Future: Instability in Europe After the Cold War." *International Security* 15, no. 1 (1990): 5–56.

O'Donnell, Guillermo, and Philippe C. Schmitter. *Transitions from Authoritarian Rule: Tentative Conclusions About Uncertain Democracies.* Baltimore: Johns Hopkins University Press, 1986.

O'Donnell, Guillermo, Philippe C. Schmitter, and Laurence Whitehead (eds.). *Transitions from Authoritarian Rule: Comparative Perspectives.* Baltimore: Johns Hopkins University Press, 1988.

Pateman, Carol. *Participation and Democratic Theory.* Cambridge: Cambridge University Press, 1970.

Pinkey, Robert. *Democracy in the Third World.* Buckingham, U.K.: Open University Press, 1993.

Pridham, Geoffrey, and Tatu Vanhanen (eds.). *Democratization in Eastern Europe: Domestic and International Perspectives.* New York: Routledge, 1994.

Przeworski, Adam. *Democracy and the Market: Political and Economic Reforms in Eastern Europe and Latin America.* Cambridge: Cambridge University Press, 1991.

Putnam, Robert D. *Making Democracy Work. Civic Traditions in Modern Italy.* Princeton: Princeton University Press, 1993.

Reiss, Hans (ed.). *Kant's Political Writings.* Cambridge: Cambridge University Press, 1970.

Risse-Kappen, Thomas. "Public Opinion, Domestic Structure, and Foreign Policy in Liberal Democracies." *World Politics* 43, no. 4 (1991): 479–513.

Rueschemeyer, Dietrich, Evelyne Huber Stephens, and John D. Stephens. *Capitalist Development and Democracy.* Cambridge: Polity Press, 1992.

Rummel, Rudolph J. "Libertarianism and International Violence." *Journal of Conflict Resolution* 27, no. 1 (1983): 27–71.

Russett, Bruce. *Grasping the Democratic Peace. Principles for a Post–Cold War World.* Princeton: Princeton University Press, 1993.

Rustow, Dankwart A. "Transitions to Democracy." *Comparative Politics* 2, no. 3 (1970): 337–365.

Singer, Max, and Aaron Wildawsky. *Zones of Peace/Zones of Turmoil.* Chatham N.J.: Chatham House, 1993.

Sirowy, Larry, and Alex Inkeles. "The Effects of Democracy on Economic Growth and Inequality: A Review." *Studies in Comparative International Development* 25, no. 1 (1990): 126–157.

Sørensen, Georg. *Democracy, Dictatorship and Development: Economic Development in Selected Regimes of the Third World.* London: Macmillan, 1991.

_____. "Democracy, Authoritarianism and State Strength." *The European Journal of Development Research* 5, no. 1 (1993): 6–34.

Van Evera, Stephen. "Primed for Peace: Europe After the Cold War." *International Security* 15, no. 3 (1990/1991): 7–57.

Weede, Erich. "Democracy and War Involvement." *Journal of Conflict Resolution* 28, no. 4 (1984): 649–664.

Zartman, William I. *Collapsed States: The Disintegration and Restoration of Legitimate Authority.* Boulder: Lynne Rienner, 1995.

□   □   □

Glossary

Absolute poverty indicates the minimum level of subsistence in a specific country. The basic human needs are not met at this level of subsistence. Disease, malnutrition, and illiteracy are common.

Anarchy is the absence of political authority. The international system is anarchic because of the absence of a central political authority above the sovereign states.

An **authoritarian developmentalist regime** is a reform-oriented system that enjoys a high degree of autonomy from vested elite interests. The regime controls a state apparatus with the bureaucratic capacity for promoting development and is run by a state elite ideologically committed to boosting economic development in terms of growth and welfare.

An **authoritarian growth regime** is an elite-dominated system focused on building a strong national economy. The long-term interests of the dominant social forces are respected, whereas the workers and peasants of the poor majority are looked to for providing the economic surplus needed to get growth under way.

The **authoritarian state elite enrichment regime** has as its main aim the enrichment of the elite who control the state. Neither economic growth nor welfare is an important goal. This type of regime is often based on autocratic rule by a supreme leader. The government of Zaire, led by Mobutu, is an example.

Civil society is the realm of social relations not regulated by the state. It includes all nonstate institutions, such as interest groups, associations, civil rights groups, and youth movements. In a totalitarian system, the state attempts to absorb civil society; in such a system, all types of organizations are under state control.

A **consociational democracy** is a type of democratic system that is characterized by mechanisms serving to promote compromise and consensus among the groups in society. Such mechanisms include federalist systems, special legislative practices, and state agencies that facilitate intergroup compromise.

A **consolidated democracy**, according to Juan Linz, is one in which none of the major political actors consider that there is any alternative to democratic processes to gain power, and no political institution or group has a claim to veto the action of democratically elected decisionmakers. In short, democracy is seen as the "only game in town."

Delegitimation must be understood against the background of legitimacy, which indicates a government's right to govern based on such criteria as popular acceptance, the constitutional process, or economic or other achievements. Dele-

159

gitimation sets in when the government can no longer point to a basis for its right to govern.

Democratic autonomy is the very broad concept of democracy set forth by David Held. It includes direct participation in local community institutions, active control of elected politicians through the party system, and social as well as economic rights to ensure adequate resources for citizens' political activity. It also foresees self-management of cooperatively owned enterprises.

Democratization refers to the process of change toward more democratic forms of rule. The first phase involves the breakdown of the nondemocratic regime. In the second phase, the elements of a democratic order are established. During the third phase, consolidation, the new democracy is further developed; eventually, democratic practices become an established part of the political culture.

Elite-dominated democracies are systems in which traditional rulers remain in control, even if pressured from below, and successfully use strategies of either compromise or force—or some mix of the two—to retain at least part of their power.

The **"end of history"** is a phrase coined by Francis Fukuyama to describe the end point of humankind's ideological evolution and the universalization of Western liberal democracy as the final form of human government.

External factors are the economic, political, ideological, and other elements that constitute the international context for the processes that take place in single countries. They often have a profound influence on those processes.

Francophone Africa is the name used to describe the countries in Africa that had been under French colonial rule and that retain special ties with France. The countries making up Francophone Africa are Mauritania, Senegal, Mali, Côte d'Ivoire, the Central African Republic, Burkina Faso, Congo, Gabon, and Cameroun.

Frozen democracies is Terry Lynn Karl's label for restricted, elite-dominated democracies that are unwilling to carry out substantive reforms that address the lot of the poor.

Globalization is the intensification of economic, social, political, and cultural relations across borders.

The Group of Seven (or G7) includes the seven most economically and militarily powerful capitalist nations: the United States, Japan, Germany, Great Britain, France, Italy, and Canada. The group meets periodically to discuss global issues.

Horizontal accountability is defined by Robert Johansen as the ability of citizens to influence the decisions that are made in neighboring societies and that directly affect them. It is achieved through democratic international institutions that guarantee rights for global minorities as well as majorities.

Idealism, in the context of this book, is the view that conflict and violence can be overcome if the world is organized according to certain ideas or principles. Harmony is possible if priority is given to the "right" ideas.

The degree of **inclusiveness** (or participation) describes the number of citizens in a society who enjoy political rights and liberties. Nondemocratic regimes may exclude the large majority of the population from participation. In democratic regimes the entire adult population enjoys the full range of rights and liberties.

Interdependence is a word used to describe situations characterized by mutual dependence between countries or among actors in different countries.

An **international society,** according to Hedley Bull and Adam Watson, is a group of states that have established by dialogue and consent common rules and institutions for the conduct of their relations, and they recognize their common interest in maintaining these arrangements.

Intrafirm trade refers to trade across national borders but between different units of the same corporation.

Liberalization is the process of increasing the possibilities for political opposition and for competition for government power. Often the first steps involve improving the possibilities for open public debate, allowing criticism of the authoritarian regime, and allowing open oppositional activity.

Mass-dominated democracies are systems in which mass actors have gained the upper hand over traditional ruling classes.

Neo-patrimonialism must be understood against the background of patrimonialism, which is the name used by Max Weber to describe any type of government that originated from a royal household and that has a ruler who treats matters of state as his or her personal affair. Present-day systems of this type, such as the system of personal rule in Africa, are examples of neo-patrimonialism.

Nomenklatura is the name of the privileged class (that is, the political, economic, and ideological elite) under the Communist system. In the former Soviet Union, the *nomenklatura* numbers about 75,000 people.

Pacific union is the name Immanuel Kant used to describe his vision of a peaceful world of democracies. The pacific union would be based on three elements: first, the mere existence of democracies with their culture of peaceful conflict resolution; second, the common moral bonds that are forged between democracies; and third, the democracies' economic cooperation toward mutual advantage.

In **patron-client relationships,** a patron provides services, rewards, or protection to a number of clients in return for their personal allegiance. The patron controls the resources; the clients are thus in a relationship of dependence.

Personal rule is the name given to the African system of government based on personal loyalty toward the leading figure of the regime, the strongman. The important positions in the state are filled with followers of the strongman. Their allegiance is reinforced by their sharing of the spoils of office.

In a system with **plural voting,** some members of the electorate have more votes than others. J. S. Mill suggested that the "wiser and more talented" should have more votes than "the ignorant and less able."

Political culture, following Samuel Huntington's definition, refers to the system of values and beliefs that defines the context and meaning of political action.

Political pacts are agreements between elite groups that restrict democracy by defining vital areas of interest for the elites. Often the elite groups will not support the new democracy unless it respects these pacts.

Polyarchy is a word used by Robert Dahl to describe systems that are called democracies in this book. Dahl outlines eight conditions that must be met in order for a system to qualify as democratic. No country satisfies all of these conditions perfectly. Therefore, Dahl uses the term polyarchy for these systems.

Realism, as used in the context of this book, is a theoretical perspective on international relations that purports to analyze the world as it really is, not as it ought to be. In the real world, conflict is imminent due to forces inherent in human nature and due to the way the world's populations have chosen to organize in the form of independent, sovereign states that respect no authority outside or above themselves.

Restricted democracies are political systems with some democratic elements but also with restrictions on competition, participation, and liberties.

A **security community,** according to Karl Deutsch, is made up of groups of people having attained a sense of community and has institutions and practices strong enough and widespread enough to assure dependable expectations of peaceful exchange among its populations. "Sense of community" is a belief that common social problems must and can be resolved by processes of peaceful exchange.

Security complex is the name used by Barry Buzan to describe a group of states whose primary security concerns are linked. Examples of security complexes are Europe, the Gulf, and South Asia.

Soft authoritarian is Chalmers Johnson's label for the Japanese democracy, which has retained some mildly authoritarian features in its governmental institutions, including single-party rule, which has been a part of the system for more than three decades, and an extremely strong and comparatively unsupervised state administration.

A **totalitarian** system is an authoritarian form of regime that is characterized by the attempt of the state to control every aspect of its citizens' lives.

□   □   □

About the Book
and Author

Is the world experiencing a "springtime of democracy," now that the Berlin Wall has crumbled and many formerly communist states have begun to reconfigure their governments and economies? And if democracy is "bursting out all over," is it doing so in a sustainable fashion? Are there pitfalls as well as positive potentials in the recent trends toward democratization?

This book examines the prospects for democracy in the world today and frames the central dilemma confronting all states touched by the process of democratization. The author clarifies the concept of democracy, shows its application in different contexts, and questions whether democratic advancement will continue—and if so, at what price. The consequences of democracy for economic development, human rights, and peaceful relations among countries are illuminated in both their positive and negative aspects.

Professor Sørensen is uniquely qualified to give students and general readers a sense of the long, slow process that democratization entails—both from the inside out (at national and local levels) and from the outside in (international causes and effects). He draws on a wealth of case studies, examples, and anecdotes to illustrate historical as well as contemporary instances of democratic transition.

Democracy, as he convincingly portrays it, is a value in itself as well as a potential promoter of peace, prosperity, and human well-being. But democracy is not inevitable, and actions at every level—from the individual to the international—are necessary to ensure that frail or "frozen" democracies do not founder and that established democracies flourish.

Georg Sørensen is professor of international politics and economics at the University of Aarhus, Denmark. He has written numerous books and articles on international relations and development issues.

Index